THE WESTMINSTER KENNEL CLUB WINNERS 1997

© 1997 by T.F.H. Publications, Inc.

Distributed in the UNITED STATES to the Pet Trade by T.F.H. Publications, Inc., One T.F.H. Plaza, Neptune City, NJ 07753; distributed in the UNITED STATES to the Bookstore and Library Trade by National Book Network, Inc. 4720 Boston Way, Lanham MD 20706; in CANADA to the Pet Trade by H & L Pet Supplies Inc., 27 Kingston Crescent, Kitchener, Ontario N2B 2T6; Rolf C. Hagen Inc., 3225 Sartelon St. Laurent-Montreal Quebec H4R 1E8; in CANADA to the Book Trade by Vanwell Publishing Ltd., 1 Northrup Crescent, St. Catharines, Ontario L2M 6P5 ; in ENGLAND by T.F.H. Publications, PO Box 15, Waterlooville PO7 6BQ; in AUSTRALIA AND THE SOUTH PACIFIC by T.F.H. (Australia), Pty. Ltd., Box 149, Brookvale 2100 N.S.W., Australia; in NEW ZEALAND by Brooklands Aquarium Ltd. 5 McGiven Drive, New Plymouth, RD1 New Zealand; in Japan by T.F.H. Publications, Japan— Jiro Tsuda, 10-12-3 Ohjidai, Sakura, Chiba 285, Japan; in SOUTH AFRICA by Lopis (Pty) Ltd., P.O. Box 39127, Booysens, 2016, Johannesburg, South Africa. Published by T.F.H. Publications, Inc.
MANUFACTURED IN THE UNITED STATES OF AMERICA
BY T.F.H. PUBLICATIONS, INC.

THE WESTMINSTER KENNEL CLUB WINNERS 1997

THE WESTMINSTER KENNEL CLUB

Andrew De Prisco, Editor

T.F.H. Publications, Inc. acknowledges the work of Isabelle Francais, our on-site photographer, whose contribution is tantamount to the success of this book. Over ninety percent of the images in this book were produced by Ms. Francais and her capable crew during the Westminster Kennel Club show.

CONTENTS

Acknowledgments

The Publisher expresses its continued thanks to the Westminster Kennel Club and the dog show that is the oldest in the world and still the most prestigious. To Chester F. Collier, President of the Westminster Kennel Club, for his personal support of this project and all the good that it does for the sport of purebred dogs.

To Rita Lynch, the Office Manager for the Westminster Kennel Club, for her year 'round support and assistance to this Editor and TFH's team. Without her professionalism and kindness, this project would not be the pleasure that it is.

To Dorie Crowe and the amazing folk at M-BF Dog Show Organization, Inc., for their cooperation and for facilitating our needs. Thanks for being so exceptional—no wonder you're the best in the business. To Sharon Curran and the staff of Madison Square Garden for their help and the "power."

To Photographers Isabelle Francais and Joseph Cirincione and their staff for making this book possible—Dorothy Draffen, Nynoska Sencion, and Matthew Seeman—they make what is an extremely stressful and difficult task seem so easy!

To Mary Bloom, our photo editor and liaison to the Westminster Kennel Club, for her continued support and friendship. This will always be our special project.

Thank you James P. Crowley, Secretary of the American Kennel Club, and his staff for providing detailed AKC records of each Best of Breed winner so that this book can provide up-to-date win records. All AKC records published in this volume come directly from the AKC and are current through January 1997.

To the DOGS and their faithful handlers for cooperating with our staff on the busiest and most exciting day of the year! Without the "winners," there could be no yearbook. You are all truly the *best*. The Publisher must apologize for those dogs not pictured this year. Unfortunately, these handlers chose not to cooperate with TFH or the Kennel Club to photograph their dogs for posterity. We are all the less for it. A listing of these dogs can be found on page 185.

Special thanks to Doug Holloway, handler of our Best in Show Standard Schnauzer, for taking the time to talk about "Pa" and sending us photographs of some of his great wins.

Finally, to the staff of TFH: Dominique De Vito, Jaime Gardner, Amy Gilbert, Stacy Kennedy and Joseph Whyte, and of course Linda Lindner for the accounting of the winners' wins.

Andrew De Prisco, Editor

T.F.H. Publications, Inc. and The Westminster Kennel Club wish to acknowledge a substantial grant from Nylabone® Products which made this commemorative endeavor possible.

Herdings Dogs being judged on Tuesday, February 11, 1997: the Breed judging of Briards, where there were 13 champions, competing under judge Stanley S. Saltzman.

Preface

For the fourth year, The Westminster Kennel Club is pleased to join T.F.H. Publications in the release of the 1997 edition of *The Westminster Kennel Club Winners*. It is our hope that this book will be an important momento of the one hundred twentieth show and will evoke the wonderful moments and memories of the event. Your support of the first two editions has encouraged us to publish this third edition. Once again, the photographs have captured the beauty and strength of the magnificent dogs that bring the excitement to Westminster.

This 1997 show, being the one hundred and twenty first consecutive show, is a matter of great pride to the members of Westminster.

Again, the show brought a total of 2,500 pure-bred AKC Champions to Madison Square Garden in New York City. They came from 47 states as well as the District of Columbia, Canada and South America. This year thousands of visitors and 360 members of the press traveled from all over the world to be present.

The competition at the breed level was keen as usual. The depth of quality of the dogs was demonstrated by the wonderful group competitions and a great Best in Show finale. The breeders and exhibitors are to be congratulated for the wonderful examples of the dogs in competition.

Chester F. Collier
President
The Westminster Kennel Club

Monday evening Group judging of the Terriers is underway as Mrs. Lydia C. Hutchinson reviews Dandie Dinmont Terrier #6 being gaited.

Mid-day judging on Monday, February 10, 1997 as the Working, Hound and Non-Sporting breeds compete for the ribbons.

Ch. Parsifal Di Casa Netzer, the first Standard Schnauzer ever to win Best in Show at the Westminster Kennel Club Dog Show 1997, photographed with judge Mrs. Dorothy Collier and handler Doug Holloway, with Westminster President Mr. Chester Collier and Show Chairman Ronald Menaker presenting the trophies. Photograph courtesy of Ashbey Photography.

Best in Show:
CH. PARSIFAL DI CASA NETZER

Sent from Italian Schnauzer breeder Gabrio Del Torre to be shown in the United States, Parsifal Di Casa Netzer became the first Schnauzer to win Best in Show at the Westminster Kennel Club. Despite greater popularity, neither the Miniature Schnauzer nor the Giant Schnauzer beat its "Standard" brethren to this distinction. Of course, the Standard Schnauzer is the most ancient of the three sizes, and in Parsifal Di Casa Netzer's case, well deserved the honor. Handled to this most distinguished victory by Doug Holloway, "Pa", as he is affectionately known, is more than head of the household, he is America's number-one show dog all-systems. Handling Schnauzers has been in the Holloway blood for years. Doug's father, the well-known judge D. Roy Holloway (and last year's Best in Show judge at Westminster), handled Schnauzers professionally for years, and Doug himself has a couple decades'

On the road to Westminster, Ch. Parsifal Di Casa Netzer handled by Doug Holloway winning Best in Show at the Greater Hickory Kennel Club, Inc. on April 7, 1996 under judge Robert A. Fisher. Photograph courtesy of Earl Graham Studios.

Best in Show at the Chester Valley Kennel Club on May 11, 1996, here's Pa handled by Rita Holloway winning under Ramone Podesta. Photograph courtesy of The Standard Image, Chuck and Sandy Tatham.

experience with this impressive breed. That Pa exhibited excellent condition and showmanship on that evening of February 11, 1997 is a polite understatement. Every judge interviewed by this editor raves about the condition and overall quality of this Schnauzer among dogs.

Roy Holloway was delighted to talk about the "great one he couldn't judge." He says that Pa has "probably the best head on a Schnauzer I've ever seen. And he's the best conditioned dog." Obviously bursting with pride for his son's win at Westminster against "the strongest Working Group I've ever seen (including the Malamute that I myself gave Best in Show to the weekend before)", Roy continues to say that the dog "couldn't have been shown better, which is a credit to Doug, of course, who did an excellent job."

Handler Doug Holloway considers Westminster to be the most important dog show in the world, and he was delighted to win the breed in 1995 under Lester R. Mapes. In the Group that night under Donald M. Booxbaum, Pa "made the cut and placed 'Group Five,'" said Doug with a smile and a sigh. That year the Group was dominated by the very popular (and finally retired) Akita. Judges around the country, however, were noticing "the fifth" place winner, and Doug received a great deal of encouragement after being seen in the final Group ring.

The following year, of course, Pa had to stay home because pa was judging Best in Show. After a year as the number-one dog in the nation, Pa emerged on the WKC '97 show with great confidence. He had the distinction of several back-to-back Best in Show weekends, including the very difficult and prestigious Springfield circuit, where Doug and Pa took an unprecedented four BIS in

Pa taking Group first under Jean Fournier at the Hendersonville Kennel Club on July 26, 1996, handled by Doug. Photograph courtesy of Earl Graham Studios.

Winning under a favorite judge Mrs. Anne Rogers Clark, Doug handled Pa to this Group first at the Talbot Kennel Club on August 16, 1996. He continued on to win Best in Show under Robert Smith. Photograph courtesy of Ashbey Photography.

a row. Also in 1996, the team won the Manatee Kennel Club under Anne Rogers Clark in Florida. The entry for Mrs. Clark was overwhelming, and she attracted every top dog in the country. The Best in Show finale that day rivaled the quality one sees at Westminster—and Doug considered this victory his most precious (prior to the Garden).

Westminster is surely a special show for the Holloways, and winning under Dorothy Collier makes the event even more unforgettable, for it was under Mrs. Collier that Pa acquired his points to finish his championship with a three-point major at the Evansville Kennel Club in March 1993. She would later award the dog Group firsts and even a couple Bests in Show along the way. For Mrs. Collier to have reviewed the dog in the Westminster Best in Show ring must have been an exhilarating experience, knowing that years ago she recognized the young dog's potential and saw him mature perfectly over the years.

Parsifal Di Casa Netzer is indeed "a judge's dog"—a headpiece more perfect than any can remember on a Schnauzer, extraordinary condition, and a strong, confident gait. The judges who have had the

Group first under Robert Forsyth at the Hatboro Dog Club Show on October 4, 1996, handled by Doug. Photograph courtesy of Bernard W. and J. Kay Kernan.

J. Donald Jones awards Pa Group first at Catonsville Kennel Club on October 12, 1996, handled by Doug. Mr. Jones was one of the first judges to appreciate Pa's greatness and has awarded him numerous Group firsts, as well as Best in Show. Photograph courtesy of Ashbey Photography.

privilege have lined up to award this dog Best in Show—he has won the honor 65 times prior to WKC. The dog was shown on a limited basis in 1994, making only about 30 shows that first year. Among the judges who have admired and awarded the dog are: J. Donald Jones, Bobby Fisher, Seaver Smith, Charles Trotter, Downing Melbourne, Anne Rogers Clark, and Burton Yamada (the breeder-judge who awarded him the Breed at WKC in 1997). Doug remembers that

Don Jones was one of the very first to appreciate the dog, and also recalls the day Mel Downing chased Pa and Doug's wife Rita across the parking lot to rave about the dog's quality.

Additionally, Pa gained the support of the whole fancy and was a popular choice at many shows. Fellow handlers Peter Green, George Ward and Ricky Chashoudian have been vocal in

Melbourne Downing has long been a fan of Pa and is shown here awarding Group first to his chosen Standard Schnauzer at the Rock Creek Kennel Club on October 13, 1996. Photograph courtesy of Bernard W. and J. Kay Kernan.

their admiration of this fabulous show dog.

Mr. Chashoudian, also a well-respected judge, remembers the first time he saw Pa in the ring: "When I first saw the dog at a show in Florida two years ago, I followed the dog back to the pen where Doug had the dogs. I asked Doug to show me the dog, and he moved him up and back. I said to Doug, 'I haven't been good to you, but you bring me this dog and I will be.' And he did, and I believe I never beat him." Doug happily took Chashoudian's advice, "This is the best dog you've ever had, a super dog!" In retrospect, he adds, "One of the best dogs ever to win Westminster."

On December 7, 1996, Pa took the Metairie Kennel Club Dog Show judged by Frank Sabella. Photograph courtesy of Luis F. Sosa.

As many would expect, Pa is already a pa himself...and has produced the number-one Standard Schnauzer bitch (and the number-two Schnauzer, second only to himself). Other breedings are planned and the expectations are high. Spring '97 marks Pa's official American retirement, but he will continue to compete on an international level, with plans to attend the World Dog Show for the next few years.

Sporting Group

Judge: Dr. Bernard E. McGivern, Jr.
Steward: Mr. Robert V. Lindsay
presenting the McGivern Challenge Bowl

Group One: Gordon Setter
CH. BIT O GOLD TITAN TREASURE

Group Two: Brittany
Ch. Brittany's Ramblin' Mr H
    Bogart JH

**Group Three: German Wire-
    haired Pointer**
Ch. Ripsnorter's Thunderhart

Group Four: Irish Setter
Ch. Qualifield's Mak'N Business

Handler: Ken Murray, CPH.

**Owners: Judy Brown, Cynthia L. Pagurski, and
Peggy Nowak.**

Breeder: Peggy Nowak.

Hound Group

Judge: Mrs. Gloria Reese
Steward: Mr. Peter R. Vanbrunt
presenting the St. Hubert's Giralda Trophy

Group One: Wirehaired Dachshund
CH. STARBARRACK MALACHITE SW

Group Two: Petit Basset Griffon Vendéen
Ch. Dehra Celestine

Group Three: Afghan Hound
Ch. Tryst Of Grandeur

Group Four: Irish Wolfhound
Ch. Triumph's Honor Of Whitehall

Handler: Robert A. Fowler.

Owner: Mrs. Alan R. Robson.

Breeder: James W. Heywood.

Working Group

Judge: Mr. Charles E. Trotter
Steward: Mr. Thomas J. Hubbard
presenting the Louis F. Bishop, III Trophy

Group One: Standard Schnauzer
CH. PARSIFAL DI CASA NETZER

Group Two: Alaskan Malamute
Ch. Nanuke's Take No Prisoners

Group Three: Bernese Mountain Dog
Ch. Nashems Taylor Maid

Group Four: Doberman Pinscher
Ch. Toledobes Serenghetti

Handler: Douglas R. Holloway, Jr.

Owner: Rita Holloway and Gabrio Del Torre.

Breeder: Gabrio Del Torre.

Terrier Group

Judge: Mrs. Lydia C. Hutchinson
Steward: Mr. Fred Wagner
presenting the William A. Rockefeller Trophy

Group One: Wire Fox Terrier
CH. RANDOM REACTION

Group Two: Bedlington Terrier
Ch. Willow Wind Money Talks

Group Three: Norfolk Terrier
Ch. Max-Well's Weatherman

Group Four: Lakeland Terrier
Ch. Revelry's Awesome Blossom

Handler: Bill McFadden.

Owner: W. James and Taffe McFadden.

Breeder: W. James and Taffe McFadden.

Toy Group

Judge: Mr. Gilbert S. Kahn
Steward: Dr. Charles M. Curry, Jr.
presenting the Walter M. Jeffords, Jr. Trophy

Group One: Japanese Chin
CH. BRIARHILL ROCK AND ROLL

Group Two: Shih Tzu
Ch. Beswicks In The Nick Of Time

Group Three: Toy Poodle
Ch. Dignity Of Jewelry House Yoko

Group Four: Cavalier King Charles
    Spaniel
Ch. Partridge Wood Laughing
    Misdemeanor

Handler: Scott Sommer.

Owner: Diane L. Meyer and Geraldine B.
    Craddock.

Breeder: Geraldine B. Craddock.

Non-Sporting Group

Judge: Mrs. Marian Mason Hodesson
Steward: Mr. James F. Stebbins
presenting the James F. Stebbins Trophy

Group One: Dalmatian
CH. SPOTLIGHT'S SPECTACULAR

Group Two: Bulldog
Ch. Cherokee Dakota Robert

Group Three: Miniature Poodle
Ch. Reignon Dassin Alexandra

Group Four: Bichon Frise
Ch. Sterling Rumor Has It

Handler: Dennis M. McCoy.

Owner: Mrs. Alan Robson.

Breeders: Stephen J. and Connie M. Wagner.

Herding Group

Judge: Mrs. Betty Moore
Steward: Mr. William H. Chisholm
presenting the Strathglass Trophy

Group One: Shetland Sheepdog
CH. ZION'S MAN ABOUT TOWN

Group Two: Border Collie
Aus-Am. Ch. Nahrof First Edition

Group Three: Pembroke Welsh Corgi
Ch. Just Enuff Of The Real Thing

Group Four: Briard
Ch. Deja Vu House On Fire

Handler: Linda Guihen.

Owner: Madeleine Griffin-Cone.

Breeder: Shirley and Stephen V. Vicchitto.

Junior Showmanship

Judge: Mr. R. Stephen Shaw
Steward: Mr. William M. Duryea, Jr.
Trophy Presenter: David Stout (1996 Best Junior Handler)

Best Junior Handler: Casandra Clark

Best Junior Handler, Casandra Clark with Siberian Husky, Ch. Kadyak's Meet The Press, owned by Ardene J. Eaton and Ron and Kathie Isenberg. Casandra is 16 years old and won over an entry of 127 Juniors entered.

Finalist #2 is Jason Lynn with Basset Hound, Ch. Craigwood's Pocket Change, owned by Jason Lynn and Sandra Campbell. Jason is 17 years old.

Finalist #3 is Erin Kerfoot with English Springer Spaniel, Ch. Genuwin Grand Finale, owned by Jeff Wallace and Erin Kerfoot. Erin is 16 years old.

Finalist #4 is Rindi Gaudet with English Spring Spaniel, Ch. Yuletide's Pocket Rocket, owned by Jeri Gilpatrick. Rindi is 17 year

Preliminary Judges were Col. Jerry H. W and Mr. Burton J. Yamada.

SPORTING DOGS

Three types of gundogs are used by the hunter in the field.

Pointers and Setters locate upland game afield for the hunter by either "pointing" the nose toward the scent, or by "setting," which is assuming a rigid stance.

Retrievers bring killed or wounded game back to the hunter.

Spaniels, long or dense-coated breeds, work close to the gun in rough cover, locating, flushing and retrieving game.

There are 26 breeds or varieties in the Sporting Group:

Brittany
Pointer
Pointer (German Shorthaired)
Pointer (German Wirehaired)
Retriever (Chesapeake Bay)
Retriever (Curly-Coated)
Retriever (Flat-Coated)
Retriever (Golden)
Retriever (Labrador)
Setter (English)
Setter (Gordon)
Setter (Irish)
Spaniel (American Water)
Spaniel (Clumber)
Spaniel (Cocker) Black
Spaniel (Cocker) A.S.C.O.B.
Spaniel (Cocker) Parti-Color
Spaniel (English Cocker)
Spaniel (English Springer)
Spaniel (Field)
Spaniel (Irish Water)
Spaniel (Sussex)
Spaniel (Welsh Springer)
Vizsla
Weimaraner
Wirehaired Pointing Griffon

BRITTANY

Ch. Brittany's Ramblin' Mr. H Bogart, JH

Breeders: Joel-Leslie Maloney and G. Ruehle. *Owner*: Jenelle Larson. By Ch. Mingodell's Ramblin' Rowdy JH ex Ch. Foxfyers Yodah's Bryttney. Born 10/13/90. Dog. *Judge*: Mrs. Elaine E. Mathis.
AKC Record: 167 Bests of Breed; 8 Group One placements.

A compact, closely knit dog of medium size, a leggy dog having the appearance, as well as the agility, of a great ground coverer. Strong, vigorous, energetic and quick of movement. In temperament, a happy, alert dog, neither aggressive nor shy.

Dogs and bitches, 17½ to 20½ inches, 30 to 40 pounds.

GROUP 2

BEST OF OPPOSITE SEX:
Ch. Mt View Precious Jem. *Owners:* Mary Ann Breininger and Jennifer Saranchak.
AWARDS OF MERIT:
Ch. Castle's Soaring High Harley JH. *Owners:* Kurt Shadbolt, I.J. and B.J. Castillo.
Ch. Twnactn Jordean All In One MH. *Owners:* Eva and Gerald Klein.
Ch. Windtuck Toby Aurand JH. *Owner:* Robert B. Aurand.

POINTER

Ch. Albelarm's Bee Serious

Breeders: Michael Zollo and Mrs. Alan Robson. *Owners*: Den and Elsa Lawler, F. DePaulo, and D. Malanga. *Handler*: Peter Green. By Ch. Windcliff Hanky Panky ex Ch. Luftnase Albelarm Bee's Knees. Born 02/24/93. Dog. *Judge*: Mrs. Constance M. Barton.
AKC Record: 202 Bests of Breed, including Westminster Kennel Club 1996; 76 Group One placements; 13 Bests in Show.

The Pointer is bred primarily for sport afield; he should unmistakably look and act the part. The Pointer's even temperament and alert good sense make him a congenial companion both in the field and in the home. He should be dignified and should never show timidity toward man or dog. Dogs, 25 to 28 inches, 55 to 75 pounds; bitches, 23 to 26 inches, 45 to 65 pounds.

BEST OF OPPOSITE SEX:
   Ch. Crosswinds Raisen A Ruckus. *Owners:* Lisa Gallizzo and Beth Ann Glashoff.
AWARDS OF MERIT:
   Ch. Tahari Seriosly Joe. *Owners:* Deeann Malanga and Frank DePaulo.
   Ch. Abelarm's Beein' Ian. *Owners:* Frank DePaulo and Judy DePaulo.
   Ch. Silent Lucidity. *Owner:* Betsy Maxton.

POINTER
(GERMAN SHORTHAIRED)

Ch. Cock O'The Walk River Delta

Breeders: M.L. and Doris Lee. *Owners*: Dr. and Mrs. J.K. Montgomery, Jr. *Handlers*: Michael and Nina Work. By Ch. Up N' Adam Cock O'The Walk ex Ch. Shannon's Riverside Ruffian. Born 11/21/92. Bitch. *Judge*: Miss Dorothy M. Macdonald.
AKC Record: 143 Bests of Breed, including Westminster Kennel Club 1996; 17 Group One placements; 1 Best in Show.

The Shorthair is a versatile hunter, an all-purpose gun dog capable of high performance in field and water. The overall picture which is created in the observer's eye is that of an aristocratic, well-balanced, symmetrical animal with conformation indicating power, endurance and agility and a look of intelligence and animation. Dogs, 23 to 25 inches, 55 to 70 pounds; bitches, 21 to 23 inches, 45 to 60 pounds.

BEST OF OPPOSITE SEX:
Ch. Minado's Parade Drum Major. Owners: Barbara and Robert Caron.
AWARDS OF MERIT:
Ch. Timber's Edge Molly McGee. Owner: Robert M. Carver.
Ch. Checksix Phantom Blitzkrieg. Owners: Colonel Nathan T. and Patte Titus.
Ch. Sergeant Shultz XIII. Owner: Richard Czeczotka.

GROUP 3

POINTER (GERMAN WIREHAIRED)

Ch. Ripsnorter's Thunderhart

Breeders: Lisa and Helen George. *Owners*: Joe and Tootie Longo and Lisa George-Clipse. *Handler*: Helen George. By Ch. Ripsnorter Aspenglow Warrior ex Ch. Ripsnorters Afarrah The Heart. Born 05/10/92. Dog. *Judge*: Miss Dorothy M. Macdonald.
AKC Record: 247 Bests of Breed, including Westminster Kennel Club 1996; 38 Group One placements; 4 Bests in Show.

The German Wirehaired Pointer is a well muscled, medium sized dog of distinctive appearance. Balanced in size and sturdily built, the breed's most distinguishing characteristics are its weather resistant, wire-like coat and its facial furnishings. Of sound, reliable temperament, the German Wirehaired Pointer is at times aloof but not unfriendly toward strangers; a loyal and affectionate companion who is eager to please and enthusiastic to learn. Dogs, 24 to 26 inches; bitches, smaller but not under 22 inches.

BEST OF OPPOSITE SEX:
Ch. ADPG Suthrn Breeze JH. *Owners:* Jean Griggs and Judith Cheshire.
AWARDS OF MERIT:
Ch. Thornwoods It Had To Be You. *Owner:* Barry A. Diehl.
Ch. Ripsnorter's Lightning Strike. *Owners:* H. Huber Jr., H. Huber III and D. Navitski.

RETRIEVER (CHESAPEAKE BAY)

Ch. Coco's Chocolate Sensation, SH

Breeder: Debra Strayer. *Owners*: D. Bleifer and S. Davis. *Handler*: Ellen Cottingham. By Ch. Chestnut Hills Stone E's Tug ex Ch. Chelsea's Bold Runner. Born 12/19/89. Bitch. *Judge*: Miss Dorothy M. Macdonald. *AKC Record:* 70 Bests of Breed; 1 Group One placement.

The Chesapeake dog should show a bright and happy disposition and an intelligent expression, with general outlines impressive and denoting a good worker. Courage, willingness to work, alertness, nose, intelligence, love of water, general quality, and, most of all, disposition should be given primary consideration in the selection and breeding of the Chesapeake Bay dog. Dogs, 23 to 26 inches, 65 to 80 pounds; bitches, 21 to 24 inches, 55 to 70 pounds.

BEST OF OPPOSITE SEX:
Ch. Chesabar's Downeast Cruiser. *Owners:* Patsy and Rudy Barber, Jr.
AWARDS OF MERIT:
Ch. Sand Bar's Last Laugh. *Owner:* Diane Kiester.
Ch. Chesabar Sinbad The Sailor. *Owner:* Larry G. Ward, Jr.
Ch. Chesabara's Gamblin Gal Gunnie. *Owner:* Adey May Dunnell.

RETRIEVER (CURLY-COATED)

Ch. Ptarmigan Gale At Riverwatch, CD

Breeder: Janean Marti. *Owners*: Gary E. and Mary Meek. By Ch. Summerwind's Charles Dickens, CD ex Ch. Ptarmigan Hard Rain Falling. Born 03/21/91. Bitch. *Judge*: Miss Dorothy M. Macdonald.
AKC Record: 263 Bests of Breed, including Westminster Kennel Club 1993, 1994, 1995 and 1996; 3 Group One placements.

A strong smart upstanding dog, showing activity, endurance and intelligence. The Curly-Coated Retriever is temperamentally easy to train. He is affectionate, enduring, hardy, and will practically live in the water. Moreover, his thick coat enables him to face the most punishing covert. He is a charming and faithful companion and an excellent guard.

BEST OF OPPOSITE SEX:
Ch. Riverwatch Desert Wind. *Owners:* Carl and Barbara Drake.
AWARD OF MERIT:
Ch. Addidas Christmas Party. *Owner:* Marci Iler.

RETRIEVER (FLAT-COATED)

Ch. Flatford Fare Forward, CD

Breeders: Mary and Marv Farwell. *Owner*: Joan B. Dever. *Handler*: Charlotte Miller. By Ch. Snowdown Canis Major, CD ex Ch. Darkside Elegant Velvet, CD. Born 09/19/93. Dog. *Judge*: Mrs. Elaine E. Mathis. *AKC Record:* 56 Bests of Breed.

The Flat-Coated Retriever is a versatile family companion hunting retriever with a happy and active demeanor, intelligent expression, and clean lines. Character is a primary and outstanding asset of the Flat-Coat. He is a responsive, loving member of the family, a versatile working dog, multi-talented, sensible, bright and tractable. As a family companion he is alert and highly intelligent; a light-hearted, affectionate and adaptable friend. He retains the qualities as well as his youthfully good-humored outlook on life into old age. Dogs, 23 to 24½ inches; bitches, 22 to 23½ inches.

BEST OF OPPOSITE SEX:
Ch. Grousemoor Hihill Q Ann Lace JH. *Owners:* Mollie and Peter Heide.
AWARDS OF MERIT:
Ch. Flatford Zues The Major God JH. *Owners:* Marvin and Mary Farwell.
Ch. Twin Oak Star of Duckacres. *Owners:* Brenda Griffin, DVM, Al Godwin and Joan Sharpe.

RETRIEVER (GOLDEN)
Ch. Goodtimes Singing In The Rain

Breeders: Cannon and Maryle Goodnight. *Owners*: Maryle Goodnight and Barbara Madrigrano. *Handler*: Nicole Madrigrano. By Ch. Asterling's Buster Keaton ex Ch. Quillmark's Spring Fling. Born 05/13/92. Bitch. *Judge*: Mrs. Elaine E. Mathis.
AKC Record: 8 Bests of Breed.

A symmetrical, powerful, active dog, sound and well put together, not clumsy nor long in the leg, displaying a kindly expression and possessing a personality that is eager, alert and self-confident. Primarily a hunting dog, he should be shown in hard working condition. In temperament, friendly, reliable, and trustworthy. Quarrelsomeness or hostility towards other dogs or people in normal situations, or an unwarranted show of timidity or nervousness, is not in keeping with Golden Retriever character. Dogs, 23 to 24 inches, 65 to 75 pounds; bitches, 21½ to 22½ inches, 55 to 65 pounds.

BEST OF OPPOSITE SEX:
    Ch. Salyran Take It To The Limit. *Owners:* Jane A. Fish, Sally Cavness and Betsy Strohl.
AWARDS OF MERIT:
    Ch. Molega's Hot Toddy. *Owners:* Paul Kouski and William and Margaret Freeburg.
    Ch. Rush Hill's Haagen-Dazs CD JH. *Owners:* Mark and Tonya Struble.
    Ch. Stillwaters Fire Up North. *Owners:* Joan Cleary and Sandy Tremblay.
    Ch. Toasty's Rock 'N Roll. *Owners:* Pamela Oxenberg and Jerome Oxenberg.

RETRIEVER (LABRADOR)

Ch. Ridge View Heartland Hit Man

Breeder: Donna Reece. *Owners:* Kevin and Sandy McCabe. *Handler:* Erin Hall. By Chablais Rhapsodie En Blue ex Ch. Pine Edge Ridge Snobear. Born 04/26/95. Dog. *Judge:* Col. Jerry H. Weiss. *AKC Record:* 28 Bests of Breed; 2 Group One placements.

The general appearance of the Labrador should be that of a strongly built, medium-sized, short-coupled dog, possessing a sound, athletic conformation that enables it to function as a retrieving gun dog, the substance and soundness to hunt waterfowl or upland game for long hours under difficult conditions, the character and quality to win in the show ring, and the temperament to be a family companion. The ideal disposition is one of a kindly, outgoing, tractable nature, eager to please and non-aggressive toward man or animal. The Labrador has much that appeals to people; his gentle ways, intelligence and adaptability make him an ideal dog. Dogs, 22½ to 24½ inches, 65 to 80 pounds; bitches, 21½ to 23½ inches, 55 to 70 pounds.

BEST OF OPPOSITE SEX:
    Ch. Chillybleak Glorious Song. *Owners:* Curt and Diane Hudson.
AWARDS OF MERIT:
    Ch Tabitha's Rollick At Carowby. *Owner:* Vicky Creamer.
    Ch. Windfall's Drambuie Smuggler. *Owners:* Charles and Susan Simpson.
    Ch. Ridge View Bleu Bunny. *Owner:* Donna Reece.

SETTER (ENGLISH)
Ch. Set'R Ridge Lookin At You Kid, JH

Breeder: Melissa Johnson. *Owners*: P.J. and John Dekker and Melissa Johnson. *Handler*: Taffe McFadden. By Ch. Set'R Ridge's Accolade In Gold ex Ch. Blueprint's Set's R Ridge's Zabri, JH. Born 03/14/92. Dog. *Judge*: Mrs. Suzanne Dillin.
AKC Record: 186 Bests of Breed, including Westminster Kennel Club 1996; 76 Group One placements; 13 Bests in Show.

An elegant, substantial and symmetrical gun dog, suggesting the ideal blend of strength, stamina, grace, and style. In temperament, gentle, affectionate, friendly, without shyness, fear or viciousness. Dogs, about 25 inches; bitches, about 24 inches.

BEST OF OPPOSITE SEX:
Ch. Lampliter Attah-Tud O'Trabeiz. *Owners*: R. Foster, DVM, M. Smith, DVM and P. Ziebart.
AWARDS OF MERIT:
Ch. Oakley's Phi Slamma Jamma. *Owner*: Jim Jannard.
Ch. Flower Of Lonesome Lane. *Owner*: Joan R. Strainer.
Ch. Reidwood Poetry In Motion. *Owners*: Nancy Warner and Clifford and Iris Reid.

SETTER (GORDON)

Ch. Bit O Gold Titan Treasure

Breeder: Peggy Nowak. *Owners*: Judy Browne, Cynthia L. Pagurski, and Peggy Nowak. *Handler*: Ken Murray, CPH. By Ch. Heavenly Current Choice ex Ch. Bit O'Gold's Bathing Buteo. Born 02/11/92. Dog. *Judge*: Mrs. Suzanne Dillin.
AKC Record: 182 Bests of Breed; 67 Group One placements; 22 Bests in Show.

The Gordon Setter is a good-sized, sturdily built, black and tan dog, well muscled, with plenty of bone and substance, but active, upstanding and stylish, appearing capable of doing a full day's work. The Gordon Setter is alert, gay, interested, and aggressive. He is fearless and willing, intelligent and capable. He is loyal and affectionate, and strong-minded enough to stand the rigors of training. Dogs, 24 to 27 inches, 55 to 80 pounds; bitches, 23 to 26 inches, 45 to 70 pounds.

GROUP 1

BEST OF OPPOSITE SEX:
    Ch. Brentwood's Bit Of Elegance. *Owners*: Chuck and Pam Krothe.
AWARDS OF MERIT:
    Ch. Rockaplentys Perfect Gentlman. *Owner*: Kathy McCord.
    Ch. Shojin's Polly Anna Of Loti. *Owners*: Peggy S. Kelley and Dee Vayda.

SETTER (IRISH)
Am/Can. Ch. Quailfield's Mak'N Business

Breeders: Patricia Nagel and S. Griffiths. *Owners*: Lana Sniderman, B. Krol, P. Nagel, R. Hill, and J. Bunch. *Handler*: William Alexander. By Ch. Meadowlark's Vindicator ex Ch. Kerry-Eire Coral Charm. Born 07/26/88. Dog. *Judge*: Mrs. Suzanne Dillin.
AKC Record: 85 Bests of Breed; 14 Group One placements; 2 Bests in Show.

GROUP 4

The Irish Setter is an active, aristocratic bird dog, rich red in color, substantial yet elegant in build. The Irish Setter has a rollicking personality. Shyness, hostility and timidity are uncharacteristic of the breed. An outgoing, stable temperament is the essence of the Irish Setter. Dogs, 27 inches, about 70 pounds; bitches, 25 inches, about 60 pounds.

BEST OF OPPOSITE SEX:
Ch. Rusticwoods Love Song. *Owners:* Marilyn T. Wade and Betty Pomeroy.
AWARDS OF MERIT:
Ch. Avon Farm Mr. Debonair. *Owner:* Leslie Russell.
Ch. Marlyn Intentional Foul. *Owner:* Marilyn D. Title.
Ch. Arista's Easy Rider. *Owners:* H.S. and K. Alexander and Rhonda and Charles De Armond.
Ch. Fieldstone Gettysburg. *Owner:* Nancy Case.

SPANIEL (AMERICAN WATER)

Ch. Kei-Rin's Marshall Dillon

Breeders: Pamela W. and Randy J. Kozak. *Owners*: Maribeth Kolarchek and Pamela Kozak. *Handler*: Richard J. Donnay. By Ch. Kei-Rin's Hawkeye ex Ch. Belle Starr Of Kei-Rin. Born 06/27/94. Dog. *Judge*: Mrs. Constance M. Barton.
AKC Record: 13 Bests of Breed.

The American Water Spaniel was developed in the United States as an all-around hunting dog, bred to retrieve from skiff or canoes and work ground with relative ease. Demeanor indicates intelligence, eagerness to please and friendly. Great energy and eagerness for the hunt yet controllable in the field. Dogs, 15 to 18 inches, 30 to 45 pounds; bitches, 15 to 18 inches, 25 to 40 pounds.

BEST OF OPPOSITE SEX:
  Ch. Shadow's Tami. *Owners:* M.C. and Lori J. Morgan Jr.
AWARD OF MERIT:
  Ch. Wish'N Well Tarheel Marksman. *Owners:* Teresa Marley and Jonne Adames.

SPANIEL (CLUMBER)

Ch. Tanelorn's Screaming Eagle

Breeders: Susan and James Stockhill. *Owners*: Jeff and Vicki Mauk. *Handler*: Timothy Thomas. By Ch. Smokerise Country Gentleman ex Leybel Perfection Personify. Born 04/04/94. Dog. *Judge*: Mr. James E. Frank.

AKC Record: 46 Bests of Breed; 2 Group One placements.

The Clumber is a long, low, heavy dog. His stature is dignified, his expression pensive, but at the same time, he shows great enthusiasm for work and play. The Clumber is a loyal and affectionate dog; sometimes reserved with strangers, but never hostile or timid. Dogs, 19 to 20 inches, 70 to 85 pounds; bitches, 17 to 19 inches, 55 to 70 pounds.

BEST OF OPPOSITE SEX:
Ch. Winsome Diamonds N Emeralds. *Owners*: Denny and Sandra R. Zogg.
AWARD OF MERIT:
Ch. Clussexx White Knuckles. *Owners*: Dennis P. Fitzpatrick, Douglas A. Johnson and M. Curtis

SPANIEL
(COCKER) A.S.C.O.B.
Ch. Kapewood's Silver Escort

Breeders: Charles Nash and Durla C. Spencer. *Owner*: Carolee Douglas. *Handler*: Vito Ciaravino. By Ch. Dynamite's Master Charge ex Ch. Barcrest Durspen's Mary Kay. Born 06/02/93. Dog. *Judge*: Mr. James E. Frank.
AKC Record: 67 Bests of Breed; 5 Group One placements.

The Cocker Spaniel is the smallest member of the Sporting Group. He is a dog capable of considerable speed, combined with great endurance. Above all he must be free and merry, sound, well balanced throughout, and in action show a keen inclination to work; equable in temperament with no suggestion of timidity. Dogs, 15 inches; bitches, 14 inches.

BEST OF OPPOSITE SEX:
    Ch. Cary's Chantilly Lace. *Owner*: Carol Papp.
AWARD OF MERIT:
    Ch. Afton's Absolut. *Owners*: Carolee Douglas and Jeanne and Christopher Silva.

SPANIEL (COCKER) PARTI-COLOR

Ch. Somerset's Wake Up Call

Breeder: Laurie Ferland. *Owner*: Laurie Ferland. *Handler*: Michelle Soave. By Ch. Shatara's The Awakening ex JPK's April Showers. Born 05/05/95. Dog. *Judge*: Mr. James E. Frank. *AKC Record:* 23 Bests of Breed.

The Cocker Spaniel is the smallest member of the Sporting Group. He is a dog capable of considerable speed, combined with great endurance. Above all he must be free and merry, sound, well balanced throughout, and in action show a keen inclination to work; equable in temperament with no suggestion of timidity. Dogs, 15 inches; bitches, 14 inches.

AWARD OF MERIT:
Ch. Brickett's Hot Wheels. *Owners:* Barbara and Gene Brickett.

SPANIEL
(ENGLISH COCKER)
Ch. Kabree Designer Genes

Breeder: Kathleen Moore. *Owner*: Andra Haasis. *Handler*: Jamie Souza. By Ch. Bolynn Star Attraction ex Ch. Kabree Marilyn Merlot. Born 08/06/93. Dog. *Judge*: Mr. James E. Frank.
AKC Record: 23 Bests of Breed; 1 Group One placement.

The English Cocker Spaniel is an active, merry sporting dog, standing well up at the withers and compactly built. He is alive with energy; his gait is powerful and frictionless, capable both of covering ground effortlessly and penetrating dense cover to flush and retrieve game. The English Cocker is merry and affectionate, of equable disposition, neither sluggish nor hyperactive, a willing worker and a faithful and engaging companion. Dogs, 16 to 17 inches, 28 to 34 pounds; bitches, 15 to 16 inches, 26 to 32 pounds.

BEST OF OPPOSITE SEX:
　　Ch. Eglefeld Passion For Lace. *Owners:* Robert and Karen Leisure.
AWARDS OF MERIT:
　　Ch. Indigo's Days Of Thunder. *Owners:* R.K. and P. Vanier and L. Dobbins.
　　Ch. Blarney's Divil Made Me Do It. *Owner:* Anita C. Berkey.
　　Ch. Canterbury's Tulipwood Sandman. *Owners:* Joann Davis and Elizabeth Ann Reifer.

SPANIEL
(ENGLISH SPRINGER)
Ch. Maidenhead's Advocate

Breeder: Bud DiDonato. *Owner*: Drew DiDonato. *Handler*: Howard Huber, Jr. By Ch. Salilyn's Condor ex Ch. Maidenhead's Jubilation. Born 02/20/92. Dog. *Judge*: Mr. James E. Frank.
AKC Record: 238 Bests of Breed; 59 Group One placements; 10 Bests in Show.

The English Springer Spaniel is a medium-size sporting dog with a neat, compact body, and a docked tail. At his best he is endowed with style, symmetry, balance, enthusiasm and is every inch a sporting dog of distinct spaniel character, combining beauty and utility. The typical Springer is friendly, eager to please, quick to learn, willing to obey. Dogs, 20 inches, 49 to 55 pounds; bitches, 19 inches.

BEST OF OPPOSITE SEX:
Ch. Sentennial's Temptation. *Owners:* J.E. Lowman and Vincent L. Hillegas.
AWARDS OF MERIT:
Ch. Southampton Secret Hello. *Owners:* Donna S. Herzig, Roberta J. Murphy and Sandra W. Logan.
Ch. Ridgewyn Legacy. *Owners:* Peter Shimmin and Gary Zayac.
Ch. Frandale's Black Magic. *Owner:* Linda LeFever.

SPANIEL (FIELD)

Ch. Bitterblue's Triple Crown, WDX, CGC, TDI

Breeder: Lynn G. Finney. *Owners*: Terry and Sharon Deputy, Lynn G. Finney, and Helga Alderfer. *Handler*: J. Ralph Alderfer. By Ch. Squier's Gen Ulysses Grant ex Ch. Bitterblue's Crown Jewel. Born 03/31/91. Dog. *Judge*: Mrs. Elaine E. Mathis.
AKC Record: 213 Bests in Breed; 5 Group One placements.

The Field Spaniel is a combination of beauty and utility. It is a well balanced, substantial hunter-companion of medium size, built for activity and endurance in heavy cover and water. It has a noble carriage; a proud but docile attitude; is sound and free-moving. Unusually docile, sensitive, fun-loving, independent and intelligent, with a great affinity for human companionship. They may be somewhat reserved in initial meetings. Dogs, 18 inches; bitches, 17 inches.

BEST OF OPPOSITE SEX:
    Ch. Cotoica's Once Is Not Enough. *Owner:* Suzanne Ward Fernau.
AWARD OF MERIT:
    Ch. Winterose Dustin Windstorm. *Owners:* Alexandra Collard and Betty R. Owen.

SPANIEL
(IRISH WATER)
Ch. MiJo's Irish Rogue, CD, JH

Breeders: Dr. Susan M. Sarracino and Robert Dehl. *Owners*: Dr. Susan M. Sarracino and Robert Dehl. By Ch. Saracen Hawkeye, JH, UD ex Ch. Saracen Irish Caper, CD, JH. Born 03/01/89. Dog. *Judge*: Mrs. Elaine E. Mathis.
AKC Record: 82 Bests of Breed.

The Irish Water Spaniel presents a picture of a smart, upstanding strongly built sporting dog. Great intelligence is combined with rugged endurance and a bold, dashing eagerness of temperament. Very alert and inquisitive, the Irish Water Spaniel is often reserved with strangers. A stable temperament is essential in a hunting dog. Dogs, 22 to 24 inches, 55 to 65 pounds; bitches, 21 to 23 inches, 45 to 58 pounds.

BEST OF OPPOSITE SEX:
Ch. Irish Mist's Memory of Kelsey. *Owners:* Linda S. and Thomas C. Deckard.
AWARD OF MERIT:
Ch. Castlehill's Airjordan O'Landacre CDX. *Owner:* Melissa McMunn.

SPANIEL (SUSSEX)

Ch. Bittersweet's Caramel Companion

Breeder: Ann S. Cummings. *Owners*: Patricia R. Hill, D. and S. Zugg, and Constance Holt-Granier. *Handler*: Constance Holt-Grainer. By Ch. Warringah's Pease Pottage ex Ch. Lexxfield Stoneyhill Lily. Born 04/13/95. Bitch. *Judge*: Mrs. Elaine E. Mathis.
AKC Record: 50 Bests of Breed; 2 Group One placements.

The Sussex Spaniel presents a long and low, rectangular and rather massive appearance coupled with free movements and nice tail action. Despite the breed's somber and serious expression, it is friendly and has a cheerful and tractable disposition. Dogs and bitches, 13 to 15 inches, 35 to 45 pounds.

BEST OF OPPOSITE SEX:
Ch. Eadwerd's Almond Joy. *Owners:* Jean Burnett and Linda Shannon.
AWARD OF MERIT:
Ch. Three D Stonecroft Endeavor. *Owners:* Erin Miller and Lindsey Miller.

SPANIEL
(WELSH SPRINGER)
Am/Can. Ch. Brafci's True Colors, CD

Breeders: Tonia and Paul Farnell. *Owner*: Marion S. Daniel. By Ch. Sylabru's Thumper ex Ch. Baraboo Sissabagama. Born 02/07/**90. Dog.** *Judge*: Mrs. Constance M. Barton.
AKC Record: 48 Bests **of Breed.**

The Welsh Springer **Spaniel** is a dog of distinct variety and ancient origin. He is an attractive dog of handy size, exhibiting substance without coarseness. The Welsh Springer Spaniel is an active dog displaying a loyal and affectionate disposition. Although reserved with strangers, he is not timid, shy nor unfriendly. To this day he remains a devoted family member and hunting companion. Dogs, 18 to 19 inches; bitches, 17 to 18 inches.

BEST OF OPPOSITE SEX:
    Ch. Saga's Orange Blossom Honey. *Owner:* Sandra Ilamanen.
AWARDS OF MERIT:
    Ch. Merry One's I'm A Stateman. *Owner:* Susan Riese.
    Ch. Royailes Kool Ham Luke. *Owners:* Nora Carlton and Andrew Carlton DVM.

VIZSLA

Ch. Sandyacre's Russet Majesty, JH

Breeders: Sharon and Dave Peck. *Owners*: Judy and Mike Barber, Deborah Clark, and Marcia Adams. *Handler*: Bobby Schoenfeld. By Ch. Sandy Acre's Russet Chief ex Ch. Russet Leather's Free Spirit. Born 09/22/93. Bitch. *Judge*: Mrs. Constance M. Barton.
AKC Record: 100 Bests of Breed, including Westminster Kennel Club 1996; 34 Group One placements; 8 Bests in Show.

The Vizsla is a medium-sized short-coated hunting dog of distinguished appearance and bearing. Robust but rather lightly built; the coat is an attractive solid golden rust. This is a dog of power and drive in the field yet a tractable and affectionate companion in the home. A natural hunter endowed with a good nose and above-average ability to take training. Lively, gentle-mannered, demonstrably affectionate and sensitive though fearless with a well developed protective instinct. Dogs, 22 to 24 inches; bitches, 21 to 23 inches.

BEST OF OPPOSITE SEX:
    Ch. Barben's Standing Ovation. *Owners*: Ben and Barbara Zahn.
AWARDS OF MERIT:
    Ch. Titan-N-Bayview's Mystry Girl JH. *Owners*: Peggy S. Davis and Lori H. Salb.
    Ch. Penlee's Leader of the Band JH. *Owners*: Kim and Saul Himmelfarb.
    Ch. Voros Vadasz Cyrus Barat JH. *Owners*: Robert and Kirsten Schick.

WEIMARANER

Ch. Wismar's Slow Gin Fizz

Breeders: Barbara Wise and Linda Springthorpe. *Owners*: Barbara and Susan Wise. By Ch. Valmar Smokey City Ultra Easy, JH ex Ch. Wismar's Mint Julep. Born 02/10/93. Bitch. *Judge*: Col. Jerry H. Weiss. *AKC Record*: 159 Bests of Breed; 17 Group One placements; 1 Best In Show.

A medium-sized gray dog with fine aristocratic features. He should present a picture of grace, speed, stamina, alertness and balance. Above all, the dog's conformation must indicate the ability to work with great speed and endurance in the field. The temperament should be friendly, fearless, alert and obedient. Dogs, 25 to 27 inches; bitches, 23 to 25 inches.

BEST OF OPPOSITE SEX:
   Ch. Ultima's Stetson V. Hufmeister. *Owners*: Tom and Teresa Hill.
AWARDS OF MERIT:
   Ch. Smoky City Harbor West Xact Cut. *Owners*: Steve and Wilma Siegel, Tom Wilson and Kelly Photopoulos.
   Ch. Aria's Allegra Of Colsidex. *Owner*: Mrs. Elaine Meader.

WIREHAIRED POINTING GRIFFON
Ch. Fireside's Rollicking Ruckus, JH

Breeder: Elaine Hunsicker. *Owners:* Joe and Marge Gryskiewicz. *Handler:* Meg Romanowski. By Ch. Echo De Saint Landry ex Ch. Diana Von Herrenhausen. Born 09/05/91. Dog. *Judge:* Col. Jerry H. Weiss. *AKC Record:* 184 Bests of Breed, including Westminster Kennel Club 1994 and 1995; 12 Group One placements; 2 Bests in Show.

Medium sized, with a noble, square-shaped head, strong of limb, bred to cover all terrain encountered by the walking hunter. His easy trainability, devotion to family, and friendly temperament endear him to all. The nickname of "supreme gundog" is well earned. The Griffon has a quick and intelligent mind and is easily trained. He is outgoing, shows a tremendous willingness to please and is trustworthy. He makes an excellent family dog as well as a meticulous hunting companion. Dogs, 22 to 24 inches; bitches, 20 to 22 inches.

BEST OF OPPOSITE SEX:
Ch. Wet Acres Agatha Frisky. *Owners:* Theodore and Linda Gagnon.
AWARD OF MERIT:
Ch. Digger Dinkum Von Hampton. *Owners:* Steve Lachance and Richard Baggenstos.

HOUND DOGS

Sporting hounds, man's indispensable partner in the pursuit of game, were developed before man came to depend on firearms. Hounds come in many sizes and shapes, bred for work with game in places as varied as the Arctic and Africa.

Basically the hounds are known by how they track game: sight or scent. Afghans, Salukis, and others of the Greyhound family locate their game by sight and with their remarkable speed run it to the ground. Others like the Foxhound, Basset or Bloodhound trail by scent, giving voice all the while so the hunter can follow. Dachshunds kill underground and Otterhounds in the water.

There are 25 breeds or varieties in the Hound Group:

Afghan Hound
Basenji
Basset Hound
Beagle, Thirteen Inch
Beagle, Fifteen Inch
Black and Tan Coonhound
Bloodhound
Borzoi
Dachshund (Longhaired)
Dachshund (Smooth)
Dachshund (Wirehaired)
Foxhound (American)
Foxhound (English)
Greyhound
Harrier
Ibizan Hound
Irish Wolfhound
Norwegian Elkhound
Otterhound
Petit Basset Griffon Vendéen
Pharaoh Hound
Rhodesian Ridgeback
Saluki
Scottish Deerhound
Whippet

AFGHAN HOUND
Ch. Tryst Of Grandeur

Breeders: Roger Rechler and Susan Sprung. *Owners:* Gregg, Scott and Todd Rechler. *Handler:* Michael Leigh Canalizo. By Ch. Triumph Of Grandeur ex Shahpphire Of Grandeur. Born 02/01/91. Bitch. *Judge:* Mrs. Glorvina R. Schwartz.

AKC Record: 458 Bests of Breed, including Westminster Kennel Club 1995, 1996; 341 Group One placements, including Westminster Kennel Club 1996; 132 Bests in Show.

GROUP 3

The Afghan Hound is an aristocrat, his whole appearance one of dignity and aloofness with no trace of plainness or coarseness. He has a proudly carried head, eyes gazing into the distance as if in memory of ages past. The striking characteristics of the breed stand out clearly, giving the Afghan Hound the appearance of what he is, a king of dogs, that has held true to tradition throughout the ages. In temperament, aloof and dignified, yet gay. Dogs, 27 inches, about 60 pounds; bitches, 25 inches; about 50 pounds.

BEST OF OPPOSITE SEX:
   Ch. Tifarah's Hi-Flying Victory. *Owner:* Janis Reital.
AWARDS OF MERIT:
   Ch. Korelec's Killimamjaro. *Owners:* James Dalton and K. Korelec.
   Ch. Ararat's As Good As Gold. *Owners:* O. Tignor, Dr. A.D. Butherus and D. and E. Martin.
   Ch. Triplicity Coltrane Blues. *Owner:* Peggy Yeloushan.

BASENJI

Ch. Reveille Boutonniere, JC

Breeder: Ms. Damara Bolte. *Owner:* Dr. Jon W. Draud. *Handlers:* Michael and Nina Work. By Ch. Juju's Pistol Pete ex Ch. Serengeti Reveille Larkspur. Born 05/14/94. Dog. *Judge:* Mr. Luc Boileau.
AKC Record: 116 Bests of Breed; 18 Group One placements.

The Basenji is a small, short haired hunting dog from Africa. Elegant and graceful, the whole demeanor is one of poise and inquiring alertness. The Basenji hunts by both sight and scent. The Basenji should not bark but is not mute. An intelligent, independent, but affectionate and alert breed. Can be aloof with strangers. Dogs, 17 inches, 24 pounds; bitches, 16 inches, 22 pounds.

BEST OF OPPOSITE SEX:
Ch. Select In The Line Of Fire. *Owners:* Jeff and Tracy Leonard, DVM.
AWARD OF MERIT:
Ch. Jasiri's Parker Steven-Son. *Owners:* L. Diamond, E. Biller and J. Jones.

BASSET HOUND

Ch. Craigwood Impressive Illusion

Breeder: Sandra H. Campbell. *Owners:* Jerry and Carol O'Bryant and Baba Monk. *Handler:* Lisa-Jane Alston Meyers. By Ch. Craigwood Solow Hobbyknox ex Ch Milldonn-Craigwood Thumbs Up. Born 06/30/92. Dog. *Judge:* Mrs. Betty-Anne Stenmark.
AKC Record: 81 Bests of Breed; 17 Group One placements; 3 Bests in Show.

The Basset Hound possesses in marked degree those characteristics which equip it admirably to follow a trail over and through difficult terrain. In temperament it is mild, never sharp or timid. It is capable of great endurance in the field and is extreme in its devotion. Dogs and bitches, not more than 14 inches.

BEST OF OPPOSITE SEX:
    Ch. Deer Hill's Great Gatsby. *Owners:* Archie and Carol Kitner.
AWARD OF MERIT:
    Ch. Lil' Creek U-Haul O'Briarcrest. *Owners:* Knox And Bette Williams.

BEAGLE,
NOT EXCEEDING 13 INCHES
Ch. Kahootz Chase Manhattan

Breeders: Reed Evans and Chris Summers. *Owners:* Carroll Diaz, M. Austin, A. Williams and J. Woods. *Handler:* Miks Kurtznor. By Ch. Shaw's Spirit Of The Chase ex Ch. Just Wright's Run To You. Born 08/02/95. Dog. *Judge:* Mr. Ralph M. Lemcke.
AKC Record: 10 Bests of Breed.

A miniature Foxhound, solid and big for his inches, with the wear-and-tear look of the hound that can last in the chase and follow his quarry to the death. Dogs and bitches, not exceeding 13 inches. The soft brown eyes of the Beagle betray his warm personality but do not instantly reveal his admirable courage and stamina. The latter qualities are especially important while the Beagle is at work in the field, but in the home no gentler, more trustworthy friend could be found.

BEST OF OPPOSITE SEX:
Ch. Durrisdeer's Coeur A La Creme. *Owner:* Patricia B. Straub.
AWARDS OF MERIT:
Ch. Beowulf Timing Is Everything. *Owners:* S. Tery Giannetti and Ted Swedella Jr.
Ch. Msbehavins Blazing Hot Wheels. *Owners:* Ross Munnerlyn and Claude and Nancy Brown.

BEAGLE,
OVER 13 INCHES BUT
NOT EXCEEDING 15 INCHES
Ch. Whiskey Creek's Headliner

Breeders: Sean Lyons and Michelle Sager. *Owners:* M. Delia and Michelle Sager. *Handler:* Michael E. Scott. By Ch. White Acres I'm Heavenly Too ex Ch. Whiskey Creek N Erin's Maddy Hays. Born 04/14/92. Dog. *Judge:* Mr. Ralph M. Lemcke
AKC Record: 256 Bests of Breed; 32 Group One placements; 3 Bests in Show.

A miniature Foxhound, solid and big for his inches, with the wear-and-tear look of the hound that can last in the chase and follow his quarry to the death. Dogs and bitches, over 13 inches but not exceeding 15 inches. The soft brown eyes of the Beagle betray his warm personality but do not instantly reveal his admirable courage and stamina. The latter qualities are especially important while the Beagle is at work in the field, but in the home no gentler, more trustworthy friend could be found.

BEST OF OPPOSITE SEX:
    Ch. Meadowland Blaze Of Cappuccino. *Owners:* Bruce and Shirley Irwin.
AWARDS OF MERIT:
    Ch. Silver Ridge Sir Spencer Star. *Owners:* Jim and Cheryl West.
    Ch. Tashwould Deja Vu. *Owners:* Carroll Diaz and Kris Bloomdahl.

BLACK AND TAN COONHOUND

Ch. Creeksides Travelin' Salesman

Breeders: Linda Pincheck and Jan Brungard. *Owners:* Linda Pincheck and Jan Brungard. *Handler:* Robert Urban. By Ch. Silver Ridge Slew Of Gold ex Ch. ElMack's Cher. Born 10/27/94. Dog. *Judge:* Mr. Ralph M. Lemcke.
AKC Record: 77 Bests of Breed; 4 Group One placements; 1 Best in Show.

The Black and Tan Coonhound is first and fundamentally a working dog, a trail and tree hound, capable of withstanding the rigors of winter, the heat of summer, and the difficult terrain over which he is called upon to work. Even temperament, outgoing and friendly. As a working scent hound, he must be able to work in close contact with other hounds. Some may be reserved but never shy or vicious. Dogs, 25 to 27 inches; bitches, 23 to 25 inches.

BEST OF OPPOSITE SEX:
Ch. Triblu's Howling Hannah. *Owner:* Corrine Dahms.
AWARDS OF MERIT:
Ch. Foxfire Scarlet Woman. *Owners:* Jason and Andrea McIlwaine.
Ch. Wyeast Wild In The Country. *Owner:* Shelley Campbell.

BLOODHOUND

Ch. Bosco Trooper Of Anderlues

Breeder: Renee Saint-Louis. *Owner:* Deborah Cool. *Handler:* Steve Aguirre. By Lyme-Ho Papilie ex Harmonie Du Houx Perce. Born 10/01/93. Dog. *Judge:* Mr. Luc Boileau.
AKC Record: 29 Bests of Breed.

The Bloodhound possesses, in a most marked degree, every point and character-istic of those dogs which hunt together by scent (Sagaces). He is very powerful, and stands over more ground than is usual with hounds of other breeds. In temperament he is extremely affectionate, neither quarrelsome with compan-ions nor with other dogs. His nature is somewhat shy, and equally sensitive to kindness or correction by his master. Dogs, 25 to 27 inches, 90 to 110 pounds; bitches, 23 to 25 inches, 80 to 100 pounds.

BEST OF OPPOSITE SEX:
    Ch. The Honey Tree's Sunflower. *Owner:* Joan Glezman.
AWARDS OF MERIT:
    Ch. Smalltown's Knotty Knoggins. *Owners:* Patricia A. Simaneck and Arlene M. Unger.
    Ch. Bigwig's Bold Advocate. *Owners:* Janis and Ian Elliot.

BORZOI

Ch. Raynbos Tsarkhan

Breeders: Roni and Jennifer Zucker. *Owners:* Roni and Jennifer Zucker. *Handler:* Jack Secrest, PHA/CPH. By Ch. Majenkir Tsuperlative ex Ch. Birchwoods Sweet Child O Mine, JC. Born 05/01/95. Dog. *Judge:* Mr. Ralph M. Lemcke.
AKC Record: 4 Bests of Breed.

The Borzoi was originally bred for the coursing of wild game on more or less open terrain, relying on sight rather than scent. The Borzoi should always possess unmistakable elegance, with flowing lines, graceful in motion and repose. Dogs, at least 28 inches, 75 to 105 pounds; bitches, at least 26 inches, 15 to 20 pounds less than dogs.

BEST OF OPPOSITE SEX:
Ch. Steppeland Katrina of Abidjan. *Owners:* Cathy A. Nasierowski and D. and C. Hamilton.
AWARDS OF MERIT:
Ch. Seabury's Lauralei. *Owner:* Jay Ito.
Ch. Tamarzi Lord Oliver Grfalcon. *Owners:* Tammy and Marilynn Lockhart and Paula Moore.
Ch. Majenkir Timotheus Seven. *Owner:* Richard E. Blodgett Jr.
Ch. Majenkir Navron Mambrino. *Owner:* Karen Staudt-Cartabona.

DACHSHUND (LONGHAIRED)

Ch. Pramada's Curmudgeon L

Breeders: Pamela and Margaret Peat. *Owners:* Drs. Mark and Patrice Parker. *Handler:* Carlos J. Puig. By Ch. Pramada's Q-Bert L. ex Ch. Boondox Lavender L. Born 12/23/91. Dog. *Judge:* Mr. Luc Boileau. *AKC Record:* 202 Bests of Breed; 22 Group One placements; 2 Bests in Show.

Low to ground, long in body and short of leg with robust muscular development, the Dachshund is well-balanced with bold and confident head carriage and intelligent, alert facial expression. His hunting spirit, good nose, loud tongue and distinctive build make him well-suited for below-ground work and for beating the bush. His keen nose gives him an advantage over most other breeds for trailing. The Dachshund is clever, lively and courageous to the point of rashness, persevering in above– and below-ground work, with all the senses well-developed. Miniatures, 11 pounds and under; standards, 16 to 32 pounds.

BEST OF OPPOSITE SEX:
    Ch. Mitzdachs Double Trouble. *Owner:* Patricia K. Prellwitz.
AWARDS OF MERIT:
    Ch. Rinac Reverend Suede Pairadox SL. *Owners:* Tim and Wendy Smythe.
    Ch. Mannequin's Bahama Bob. *Owners:* Marge Chidester and Glenna Chidester.
    Ch. Walmar's Jazz Man. *Owners:* Walter and Mary Jones.

DACHSHUND (SMOOTH)

Ch. Forrester's Hunter

Breeders: Frances and James Forrester. *Owners:* Frances and James Forrester. *Handler:* Patrick Willer. By Ch. Laddland A Wing & A Prayer ex Ch. Forrester's Lady In Red. Born 10/23/92. Dog. *Judge:* Mr. Luc Boileau. *AKC Record:* 102 Bests of Breed; 7 Group One placements.

Low to ground, long in body and short of leg with robust muscular development, the Dachshund is well-balanced with bold and confident head carriage and intelligent, alert facial expression. His hunting spirit, good nose, loud tongue and distinctive build make him well-suited for below-ground work and for beating the bush. His keen nose gives him an advantage over most other breeds for trailing. The Dachshund is clever, lively and courageous to the point of rashness, persevering in above– and below-ground work, with all the senses well-developed. Miniatures, 11 pounds and under; standards, 16 to 32 pounds.

BEST OF OPPOSITE SEX:
 Ch. Galadachs Sunkissed. *Owner:* Eric Henningsen.
AWARDS OF MERIT:
 Ch. Landmark Simone V. Joyal. *Owners:* Barbara L. Powers, Anne A. Crockett amnd Nancy C. Weber.
 Ch. Dachsmith Love's Ajax. *Owners:* Iris Love and Liz Smith.
 Ch. Cedarcreek's Bold Sojer Boy. *Owners:* Larry J. and Rebecca Payne.

DACHSHUND (WIREHAIRED)

Ch. Starbarrack Malachite SW

Breeder: James W. Heywood. *Owner:* Mrs. Alan R. Robson. *Handler:* Robert Fowler. By Ch. Saytar's Little Bohannon SW ex Ch. Fancy That Amalia SW. Born 02/07/91. Dog. *Judge:* Mr. Luc Boileau.
AKC Record: 368 Bests of Breed, including Westminster Kennel Club 1993; 104 Group One placements; 25 Bests in Show.

GROUP 1

Low to ground, long in body and short of leg with robust muscular development, the Dachshund is well-balanced with bold and confident head carriage and intelligent, alert facial expression. His hunting spirit, good nose, loud tongue and distinctive build make him well-suited for below-ground work and for beating the bush. His keen nose gives him an advantage over most other breeds for trailing. The Dachshund is clever, lively and courageous to the point of rashness, persevering in above- and below-ground work, with all the senses well-developed. Miniatures, 11 pounds and under; standards, 16 to 32 pounds.

BEST OF OPPOSITE SEX:
Ch. J's Lesiel's Luv Bug. *Owner:* Sharon B. Johnson.
AWARDS OF MERIT:
Ch. Westphals Highway Run. *Owner:* Peggy A. Westphal.
Ch. Rose Farm's Calcide SW. *Owner:* Vera Falco.
Ch. Brazos Ski Flower Bar The Doo. *Owners:* Kelli Williams and Drs. Mark and Patrice Parker.

FOXHOUND (AMERICAN)

Ch. Kelly Mt. Prime Time

Breeder: J.R. Hicks. Owners: James M. and Judy G. Rea. *Handler:* James M. Rea. By Sand Mtn. Train ex Sand Mtn. Kitty. Born 02/03/90. Dog. *Judge:* Mr. Ralph M. Lemcke.
AKC Record: 323 Bests of Breed, including Westminster Kennel Club 1994 and 1995; 44 Group One placements; 8 Bests in Show.

The vital characteristics of any Foxhound are: quality, neither coarse nor overre-fined; proper structure, resulting in balance; and activity, based on movement—careful observation of the initial stride often provides the clue. These are essentially packhounds that are docile and friendly, though not overly demonstrative to people; not good family pets, they are rapacious hunting hounds born and bred to follow a scent and they thrive on outdoor kennel life. Dogs, 22 to 25 inches; bitches, 21 to 24 inches.

BEST OF OPPOSITE SEX:
Ch. Devlon's Hard Headed Woman. *Owners:* Donald and Kelly Leonard and Kristen Kendall.
AWARD OF MERIT:
Ch. K-Phil's Lead On. *Owners:* Helen C. Greene and Kay Phillips.

FOXHOUND (ENGLISH)

Ch. Casualeigh Liaison

Breeder: L.R. Gibson, Jr. *Owners:* Michelle Sager and Tony Castellano. *Handler:* Michael E. Scott. By Casualeigh Water Mark ex Casualeigh Lyric. Born 09/02/90. Dog. *Judge:* Mr. Ralph M. Lemcke.
AKC Record: 42 Bests of Breed; 7 Group One placements; 1 Best in Show.

In general appearance, a balanced, symmetrical hound, selected for scenting power, cry, drive, stamina, moderate speed, pack sense and courage. Variation among different packs has been selected for functionally and is based on differences in regional ecologies.

In temperament, an intelligent, courageous pack hound of cheerful, determined disposition. Dogs and bitches, 24 inches.

BEST OF OPPOSITE SEX:
Ch. Sunup's Victoria. *Owner:* Sue N. Whaley.
AWARD OF MERIT:
Ch. Sunyo's Blue Ribbon. *Owners:* Giselle Sasker and Sue N. Whaley.

GREYHOUND

Ch. Shazam's The Journey Begins

Breeders: Jack E. and Margaret S. Mitchell. *Owners:* Kim Fritzler, Jack Mitchel and Brad Child. *Handler:* Kim Fritzler. By Ch. Jets The Voyage Out ex Ch. Gallant Somnombula. Born 06/05/92. Dog. *Judge:* Mr. Ralph M. Lemcke.
AKC Record: 80 Bests of Breed; 11 Group One placements; 3 Bests in Show.

Strongly built, upstanding, of generous proportions, elegant, muscular, powerful and symmetrical formation; possessing remarkable stamina and endurance; intelligent, gentle, very affectionate and even tempered. Greyhounds make quiet housedogs and are easily socialized; they are not as shy and retiring as one might expect and do not require a large home to dwell contentedly. Dogs, 65 to 70 pounds; bitches, 60 to 65 pounds.

BEST OF OPPOSITE SEX:
    Ch. Jets Ravishing Red Head. *Owner:* Geri Ann Etheridge.
AWARDS OF MERIT:
    Ch. Huzzah Red Alert. *Owners:* L.S. Richer and Dr. G. Nash.
    Ch. Gerico's Chasing The Wind. *Owner:* Geri Ann Etheridge.

HARRIER

Ch. Kingsbury Pacific Ring Of Fire

Breeder: Donna K. Smiley-Auborn. *Owners:* Helen Cacciottoli, K. Crary, and Dr. G. Nash. *Handler:* Greg Myers. By Ch. Rockwood Hardwick, CD ex Ch. Hartshire's Indoor Fireworks, CD. Born 04/24/93. Dog. *Judge:* Mr. James R. White.
AKC Record: 210 Bests of Breed; 15 Group One placements.

Developed in England to hunt hare in packs, Harriers must have all the attributes of a scenting pack hound. They must be active, well balanced, full of strength and quality, in all ways appearing able to work tirelessly, no matter the terrain, for long periods. Outgoing and friendly, as a working pack breed, Harriers must be able to work in close contact with other hounds. Therefore, aggressiveness towards other dogs cannot be tolerated. Dogs and bitches, 19 to 21 inches.

BEST OF OPPOSITE SEX:
Ch. Wesford's Scent Of A Fool. *Owner:* Lisa and Michael Perez.
AWARD OF MERIT:
Ch. Wesford's Never Look Back. *Owners:* Kimberly G. Mitchell and Denise E. Brown.

IBIZAN HOUND

Ch. Hemato's J-Mark Star Maiden

Breeders: Mary L. Toliver and Jim S. Porcher. *Owner:* Jeffrey M. Macek. *Handler:* Pamela Lambie, PHA. By Ch. Paradise Legacy O'Bramblwood ex Ch. Paran Cast A Spell. Born 11/23/93. Bitch. *Judge:* Mr. James R. White.
AKC Record: 67 Bests of Breed; 2 Group One placements.

A hunting dog whose quarry is primarily rabbits, this ancient hound was bred for thousands of years with function being of prime importance. Lithe and racy, the Ibizan possesses a deerlike elegance combined with the power of a hunter. The Ibizan is even-tempered, affectionate and loyal. Extremely versatile and trainable, he makes an excellent family pet and is well suited to the breed ring, obedience, tracking and lure-coursing. He exhibits a keen, natural hunting instinct with much determination and stamina in the field. Dogs, 23½ to 27½ inches, 50 pounds; bitches, 22 ½ to 26 inches, 45 pounds.

BEST OF OPPOSITE SEX:
Ch. Mentors Arirzes Betsy's Boy. *Owner:* John H. Mentzer.
AWARD OF MERIT:
Ch. Bramblewood Taali' Of Husn. *Owner:* Carol Dickerson Kauffman.

IRISH WOLFHOUND

Ch. Triumph's Honor Of Whitehall

Breeders: Mr. and Mrs. Frank R. Dean, Jr. *Owners:* Mr. and Mrs. Frank R. Dean, Jr. By Ch. Marcmora Fame's Triumph ex Ch. Fleetwind Voodoo Of Whitehall. Born 03/31/92. Dog. *Judge:* Mr. James R. White. *AKC Record:* 112 Bests of Breed; 14 Group One placements.

Of great size and commanding appearance, the Irish Wolfhound is remarkable in combining power and swiftness with keen sight. The largest and tallest of the galloping hounds, in general type he is a rough-coated Greyhoundlike breed. Dogs, minimum of 32 inches and 120 pounds; bitches, minimum of 30 inches and 105 pounds.

GROUP 4

BEST OF OPPOSITE SEX:
   Ch. Corcra Gael Sionnach Of Eagle. *Owner:* Gael Lewis Damron.
AWARDS OF MERIT:
   Ch. Nutstown Fear Mor of St. Doulaghs JC. *Owners:* Eileen M. and
      Eileen B. Flanagan.
   Ch. Riverlawn Maestro Of Eagle. *Owners:* Dennis and Anne Gallant
      and Samuel Evans Ewing III.

NORWEGIAN ELKHOUND
Ch. Hayfield's New Locomotion

Breeder: Mary J. New. *Owner:* Rev. Dr. Abraham E. New. *Handlers:* Michael and Nina Work. By Ch. Hojo's Mountain Hunter ex Ch. Hayfield's Silver Katrina. Born 07/07/92. Dog. *Judge:* Mr. James R. White. *AKC Record:* 87 Bests of Breed; 3 Group One placements.

The Norwegian Elkhound is a hardy gray hunting dog, a square and athletic member of the northern dog family. His unique coloring, weather resistant coat and stable disposition make him an ideal multipurpose dog at work and play. In temperament, the Norwegian Elkhound is bold and energetic, an effective guardian yet normally friendly, with great dignity and independence of character. Dogs, 20½ inches, about 55 pounds; bitches, 19½ inches, about 48 pounds.

BEST OF OPPOSITE SEX:
Ch. Vin-Melca's Patchwork. *Owners:* Sigurd and K. Harbark.
AWARD OF MERIT:
Ch. Arjess Sit'n On A Gold Mine. *Owners:* Roberta Jean Sladeck and Sandi Peterson.

OTTERHOUND

Ch. Aberdeen's Caveman

Breeders: Andrea and Jack McIlwaine. *Owners:* Betsy Maxton and Andrea and Jack McIlwaine. *Handler:* Mike Szabo. By Ch. Scentasia's Doonesbury ex Ch. Aberdeen's Alien. Born 06/11/91. Dog. *Judge:* Mr. James R. White.
AKC Record: 238 Bests of Breed; 16 Group One placements.

The Otterhound is a large, rough-coated hound with an imposing head showing great strength and dignity, and the strong body and long striding action fit for a long day's work. It has an extremely sensitive nose, and is inquisitive and perseverant in investigating scents. The Otterhound hunts its quarry on land and water and requires a combination of characteristics unique among hounds. The Otterhound is amiable, boisterous and even-tempered. Dogs, 24 to 27 inches, 75 to 115 pounds; bitches, 23 to 26 inches, 65 to 100 pounds.

BEST OF OPPOSITE SEX:
Ch. Hooters Mrs. Snuggle Puss. *Owners:* Dr. Carol B. Gilmore and Sandy M. Burns.
AWARD OF MERIT:
Ch. Aberdeen Bently O'Corcra Gael. *Owner:* Gael Lewis Damron.

GROUP 2

PETIT BASSET GRIF-FON VENDÉEN

Ch. Dehra Celestine

Breeder: Nicholas Frost. *Owners:* Mr. and Mrs. Nicholas Frost and Mr. and Mrs. P. Kovar. *Handler:* Michael E. Scott. By Jomil Zadok ex Dehra Psyche. Born 02/19/93. Bitch. *Judge:* Mr. James R. White.
AKC Record: 67 Bests of Breed; 16 Group One placements; 2 Bests in Show.

The Petit Basset Griffon Vendéen is a scent hound developed to hunt small game over the rough and difficult terrain of the Vendéen region. He is bold and vivacious in character; compact, tough and robust in construction. He has an alert outlook, lively bearing and a good voice freely used. In temperament, happy, extroverted, independent, yet willing to please. Dogs and bitches, 13 to 15 inches.

BEST OF OPPOSITE SEX:
Ch. Charlen's For You Eyes Only. *Owners:* Linda Kendall and Charles and Helen Ingher.
AWARDS OF MERIT:
Ch. Tip-Top's Little Big Man. *Owners:* Linda and Chris Taranto and Helen Ingher.
Ch. Pepperhill's O'Henri. *Owners:* Jeff and Barbara Pepper.

PHARAOH HOUND
Ch. Enigma Sweet Heather-Bell

Breeder: Madelene Lonn. *Owners:* Nancy and Bill Sowerbutts. *Handler:* Rebecca Lockhart. By Antefa's Jabbah-Kaa ex Enigma Sophia. Born 05/19/93. Bitch *Judge:* Mrs. Elaine Rigden. *AKC Record:* 60 Bests of Breed; 1 Group One placement.

General appearance is one of grace, power and speed. The Pharaoh Hound is medium sized, of noble bearing with hard clean-cut lines—graceful, well balanced, very fast with free easy movement and alert expression. Intelligent, friendly, affectionate, playful and active. Very fast with a marked keenness for hunting, both by sight and scent. Dogs, 23 to 25 inches; bitches, 21 to 24 inches.

BEST OF OPPOSITE SEX:
   Ch. Merymut Neferkare. *Owner:* Marilyn M. Smith.
AWARD OF MERIT:
   Ch. Kamaraj Bija Ka-Harakhty. *Owners:* Marilyn Smth and
      Margaret Worth.

RHODESIAN RIDGEBACK

Ch. Deer Ridge Sea King

Breeders: Linda and Shirley Batson. *Owners:* Greg Louganis, Linda and Shirley Batson, and David Bueno. By Ch. Calico Ridge Jolly Roger ex Deer Ridge Snappy Ginger. Born 04/06/94. Dog. *Judge:* Mrs. Elaine Rigden. *AKC Record:* 29 Bests of Breed; 4 Group One placements.

The Ridgeback should represent a strong muscular and active dog, symmetrical in outline, and capable of great endurance with a fair amount of speed. The peculiarity of this breed is the ridge on the back, which is formed by the hair growing in the opposite direction to the rest of the coat. A member of the hound family, the Ridgeback is strong-minded and re-served. He can be aggressive with other dogs. He is a splendid companion—obedience training is essential. This is a natural and serious hunter. Dogs, 25 to 27 inches, 75 pounds; bitches, 24 to 26 inches, 65 pounds.

BEST OF OPPOSITE SEX:
Ch. Penelope II. *Owner:* Robert L. Russell.
AWARDS OF MERIT:
Ch. Riveroads Jhusta Sweet Reward. *Owners:* Bruno and Mary Ann Mauer.
Ch. Ridgelea's Lord Reading. *Owners:* Dr. Michael and Barbara Golfarb.
Ch. Wheatridge Kahlu Hurricane Darla. *Owners:* Pat Brunstetter and Katherine Stein.
Ch. Filmaker's Never Surrender Of FM JC. *Owners:* Frank and Judy DePaulo.
Ch. Clapton Z Masai. *Owner:* John F. Rodgers.

SALUKI

Ch. Windstorm Luck Be A Lady

Breeders: Randy and Starr White. *Owners:* Randy and Starr White. *Handlers:* William and Allison Alexander. By Ch. Clarinda Sunna Sarea Bashir ex Ch. Windstorm Melik Gillian. Born 07/03/93. Bitch. *Judge:* Mrs. Elaine Rigden.
AKC Record: 1 Best of Breed.

The whole appearance of this breed should give an impression of grace and symmetry and of great speed and endurance coupled with strength and activity to enable it to kill gazelle or other quarry over deep sand or rocky mountains. The expression should be dignified and gentle with deep, faithful, far-seeing eyes. Dogs, 23 to 28 inches; bitches, considerably smaller.

BEST OF OPPOSITE SEX:
Ch. Ariel Sonova Drama Of Hasten. *Owner:* Cheryl R. Rosenberger.
AWARDS OF MERIT:
Ch. Abu Simbel Desert Phantom. *Owner:* Sarah, Denise and Barry J. Edelman MD.
Ch. Ranesaw Imperial Beach JC. *Owners:* Harry Stiles, Lee Walker and J. Wassenaar.

SCOTTISH DEERHOUND
Ch. Upland's Liam Of Quaker Hill

Breeders: Dru and Steve Pollinger. *Owners:* Virginia and John T. Hogan. By Ballantine D'Lux Of Fair Haven ex Fearnwood Ayla. Born 07/07/89. Dog. *Judge:* Mrs. Elaine Rigden.
AKC Record: 41 Bests of Breed; 10 Group One placements; 3 Bests in Show.

A typical Deerhound should resemble a rough-coated Greyhound of larger size and bone. As tall as possible without losing quality. Dogs, 30 to 32 inches and up; bitches, 28 inches and up.

BEST OF OPPOSITE SEX:
    Ch. Aberdeen's Ikea Of Vale Vue. *Owner:* Thomas J. Gentner.
AWARD OF MERIT:
    Ch. Sindar's Mega Buck. *Owner:* Rachael Matthews.

WHIPPET

Ch. Patric's Personal Aggenda

Breeder: Patrick J. Pettit. *Owners:* Patrick J. Pettit and Pennyworth Kennels. *Handler:* Claire Newcombe. By Ch. Chelsea Legerdemain ex Ch. Patric's Except No Substitute. Born 09/28/94. Bitch. *Judge:* Mrs. Elaine Rigden.
AKC Record: 41 Bests of Breed; 10 Group One placements; 3 Bests in Show.

A medium size sighthound giving the appearance of elegance and fitness, denoting great speed, power and balance without coarseness. A true sporting hound that covers a maximum of distance with a minimum of lost motion. Amiable, friendly, gentle, but capable of great intensity during sporting pursuits. Dogs, 19 to 22 inches; bitches, 18 to 21 inches.

BEST OF OPPOSITE SEX:
Ch. Sporting Fields Kinsman. *Owners:* Mrs. James Butt, Dionne E. Butt, and E. Hansen.
AWARDS OF MERIT:
Ch. Surrey Hill's Sanibel Sand SC. *Owners:* Saulo Jr. P. Biscoto, Karen Bowers Lee and Carolyn Bowers.
Ch. Norika's Pretty Woman. *Owners:* Geraldine L. Putnam and Bente Opsahl.

WORKING DOGS

Although these breeds are sometimes expected to double as hunters, their principal service has been to assist man in his daily work. They have traditionally guarded man's home and his stock, served as drovers, all-around farm dogs and draft animals. Today they also serve as guard dogs, police and border patrol dogs, guide dogs for the blind and dogs of war.

Because of the wide variety of uses for the dogs in this group, there are great differences in appearance. Most, however, are powerfully built and unusually intelligent.

There are 20 breeds in the Working Group:

Akita
Alaskan Malamute
Bernese Mountain Dog
Boxer
Bullmastiff
Doberman Pinscher
Giant Schnauzer
Great Dane
Great Pyrenees
Greater Swiss Mountain Dog
Komondor
Kuvasz
Mastiff
Newfoundland
Portuguese Water Dog
Rottweiler
Saint Bernard
Samoyed
Siberian Husky
Standard Schnauzer

AKITA

Ch. T'stone's The Hustler

Breeders: Pamela Deming, Josh Rossi and Julie Hoehn. *Owners:* Pamela Demins, Sylvia Thomas and Geno Relampagos. *Handler:* Bruce Schultz, CPH/PHA. By Ch. Goshen Lethal Weapon ex Fair Winds Hearts On Fire. Born 03/12/93. Dog. *Judge:* Mr. Burton J. Yamada.

AKC Record: 36 Bests of Breeds; 3 Group One placements.

Large, powerful, alert, with much substance and heavy bone. Alert and responsive, dignified and courageous. Aggressive toward other dogs. Dogs, 26 to 28 inches; bitches, 24 to 26 inches.

BEST OF OPPOSITE SEX:
    Ch. Ajado's Hugs N Kisses To Toh. *Owners:* Mary Ann Brewer and
        Donna M. Trenkler-Percivalle.
AWARDS OF MERIT:
    Ch. Hinomaru Inazuma-Tatsumaki. *Owners:* Stephen and Sharon
        Gignilliat and Wallace Smith.
    Ch. North Star's Sabre Saw. *Owners:* K. Burland, A. Weatherman, and
        K. Levesque.
    Ch. The Joker is Wild O'BJ. *Owners:* Lillian Kletter and Laura Payton.
    Ch. Apogee's Back to the Future. *Owners:* Beth L. Elliott, L. Snickles,
        and P. Bruneau.

GROUP 2

ALASKAN MALAMUTE

Ch. Nanuke's Take No Prisoners

Breeders: Sandra and Rose Marie D'Andrea. *Owners:* Kathleen P. Leuer and Sandra D'Andrea. By Ch. Nanuke's Revolutionary ex Ch. Nanuke's Seal Of Approval. Born 04/17/93. Dog. *Judge:* Mr. Burton J. Yamada.
AKC Record: 124 Bests of Breed, including Westminster Kennel Club 1996; 56 Group One placements; 23 Bests in Show.

The Alaskan Malamute is a powerful and substantially built dog with a deep chest and strong, compact body. The Alaskan Malamute is an affectionate, friendly dog, not a "one-man" dog. He is a loyal, devoted companion, playful on invitation, but generally impressive by his dignity after maturity. The Malamute as a sledge dog for heavy freighting is designed for strength and endurance. Dogs, 25 inches, 85 pounds; bitches, 23 inches, 75 pounds.

BEST OF OPPOSITE SEX:
Ch. Kohoutec Willow Ptarmigan. *Owners:* Dennis E. Collins and Robert McCullough

BERNESE MOUNTAIN DOG

GROUP 3

Ch. Nashems Taylor Maid

Breeder: Sara Karl. *Owners:* Sara and Randall Karl and Ruth Cooper. By Ch. De-Li's Standing Ovation ex Ch. Nashems Becken V Woodmoor, CD. Born 11/29/93. Bitch. *Judge:* Mrs. Lynette J. Saltzman.
AKC Record: 116 Bests of Breed, including Westminster Kennel Club 1996; 19 Group One placements; 8 Bests in Show.

The Bernese Mountain Dog is a striking, tri-colored, large dog. He is sturdy and balanced. He is intelligent, strong and agile enough to do the draft and droving work for which he was used in the mountainous regions of his origin. The temperament is self-confident, alert and good natured, never sharp or shy.

The Bernese Mountain Dog should stand steady, though may remain aloof to attentions of strangers. Dogs, 25 to 27½ inches; bitches, 23 to 26 inches.

BEST OF OPPOSITE SEX:
    Ch. De-Li's Chain Reaction. *Owner:* Lilian Ostermiller.
AWARDS OF MERIT:
    Ch. Degrasso's Griffiths V. Legacy. *Owner:* Heather Bremmer.
    Ch. Snobear's Gambling Fool. *Owner:* Linda Morton.
    Ch. Bev's Royal Sun Fendi V. BB. *Owners:* Beverly Burney and William Burney.

BOXER

Ch. Vancroft's Primetime

Breeders: Deborah Clark, Marcia Adams, and Jimmy Sawyers. *Owners:* Deborah Clark and Marcia Adams. *Handlers:* Bobby Schoenfeld and Kay Palade. By Ch. Misty Valley's Curtain Call ex Ch. Vancroft's Vogue. Born 06/07/91. Dog. *Judge:* Mrs. Marcia P. Tucker.
AKC Record: 218 Bests of Breed; 41 Group One placements; 5 Bests in Show.

Developed to serve as guard, working and companion dog, the Boxer combines strength and agility with elegance and style. His expression is alert and temperament steadfast and tractable. Instinctively a "hearing" guard dog, his bearing is alert, dignified and self-assured. With family and friends, his temperament is fundamentally playful, yet patient and stoical with children. Deliberate and wary with strangers, he will exhibit curiosity but, most importantly, fearless courage if threatened. However, he responds promptly to friendly overtures honestly rendered. His intelligence, loyal affection and tractability to discipline make him a highly desirable companion. Dogs, 22½ to 25 inches; bitches, 21 to 23½ inches.

BEST OF OPPOSITE SEX:
Ch. Huffand's Obladah Of Arriba. *Owners:* P. Koenig, B. Greenberg and B. Gibson.
AWARDS OF MERIT:
Ch. Sirrocco's Kiss By The Book. *Owners:* Ray Culberson, Bill Weber and Diane Mallet.
Ch. Winmor's Wild Irish Rose. *Owners:* Jane Wilkinson, Ellen Bradley and Kathy Frohock.
Ch. Crossroad's PVS On My Honor. *Owners:* B. Williams, T. and J. Self, D. Hart and R. Appleby.
Ch. Hi-Tech Johnny J of Boxerton. *Owners:* Dr. William Truesdale and Zoila Truesdale.

BULLMASTIFF
Ch. Avonlea Storybook Goodfella

Breeders: Karen Skiba and Helen Nietsch. *Owner:* Deborah J. Gannett. *Handler:* Carol A. Nock. By Ch. Allstar's Mugsy Malone ex Banstock Paige Of Shady Oak. Born 04/07/94. Dog. Judge: Mrs. James Edward Clark.
AKC Record: 9 Bests of Breed.

In general appearance, that of a symmetrical animal, showing great strength, endurance, and alertness; powerfully built but active. The foundation breeding was 60% Mastiff and 40% Bulldog. The breed was developed in England by gamekeepers for protection against poachers. Fearless and confident yet docile. The dog combines the reliability, intelligence, and willingness to please required in a dependable family companion and protector. Dogs, 25 to 27 inches, 110 to 130 pounds; bitches, 24 to 26 inches, 100 to 120 pounds.

BEST OF OPPOSITE SEX:
  Ch. Leathernecks LivnOn Tulsatine. *Owners:* Bob and Lynn Spohr and
      Perry Payson.
AWARDS OF MERIT:
  Ch. Leatherneck's Grizzley. *Owners:* Anita D. Lewis and Angie Reese.
  Ch . Blazins The Buck Stops Here. *Owners:* Deborah M. Worrell and
      Tom and Roxanne LaPaglia.
  Ch. Ladybug Thorn Of The Rosebd. *Owners:* Peggy Ann Graham and
      Fred and Candy Welch.
  Ch. Gra-Wel's Bourbon Queen. *Owners:* Peggy A. Graham and Candy Welch.
  Ch. Beowulf Glory Girl. *Owners:* Jenny Baum and Nick Douglas.

GROUP 4

DOBERMAN PINSCHER

Ch. Toledobes Serenghetti

Breeders: Sue Brown, Judy Doniere and Barbara Randall. *Owners:* H. and H. Hedinger and R. and S. Johnson. Handler: Andy Linton. By Ch. Lancaster's Courvosier ex Ch. Toledobes Caught Cheating. Born 04/18/94. Bitch. *Judge:* Mrs. Marcia P. Tucker.
AKC Record: 155 Bests of Breed; 101 Group One placements; 46 Bests in Show.

The appearance is that of a dog of medium size, with a body that is square. Compactly built, muscular and powerful, for great endurance and speed. Elegant in appearance, of proud carriage, reflecting great nobility and temperament. Energetic, watchful, determined, alert, fearless, loyal and obedient. Dogs, ideally 27½ inches; bitches, ideally 25½ inches.

BEST OF OPPOSITE SEX:
    Ch. V. Ragus NX Generation Manarjj. *Owners:* Jim and Nancy Barrett.
AWARDS OF MERIT:
    Ch. Cambria's Carman. *Owner:* Judy A. King.
    Ch. Lancaster Lord And Taylor. *Owners:* R. and A. Saliba.

GIANT SCHNAUZER

Ch. Skansen's Sixty Minutes

Breeder: Sylvia Hammarstrom. *Owners:* Dr. and Mrs. William Truesdale and Mr. and Mrs. K. Greenslade. *Handler:* Kimberly Pastella. By Ch. Lucas De Campos De Oro ex Ch. Skansen's Old Spice. Born 02/04/94. Bitch. *Judge:* Mr. James R. White.
AKC Record: 108 Bests of Breed; 22 Group One placements; 2 Bests in Show.

The Giant Schnauzer should resemble, as nearly as possible, in general appearance, a larger and more powerful version of the Standard Schnauzer, on the whole a bold and valiant figure of a dog. Robust, strongly built, nearly square in proportion of body length to height at withers, active, sturdy and well muscled. Temperament combines spirit and alertness with intelligence and reliability. Composed, watchful, courageous, easily trained, deeply loyal to family, playful, amiable in repose, and a commanding figure when aroused. The sound, reliable temperament, rugged build, and dense weather-resistant wiry coat make for one of the most useful, powerful, and enduring working breeds. Dogs, 25½ to 27½ inches; bitches, 23½ to 25½ inches.

BEST OF OPPOSITE SEX:
Ch. Skansen's Rembrandt II. *Owners:* Mickey and Linda Low.
AWARDS OF MERIT:
Ch. Ruster's Your Cheatin' Heart. *Owners:* Samuel B. and Marion W. Lawrence.
Ch. Skansen's Che Sara Sara. *Owner:* Michelle Kogut.

GREAT DANE

Ch. Harley Davidson Hardt's

Breeder: Tonie Gerhardt. *Owners:* Stephanie Gallups and Tonie Gerhardt. *Handler:* Terry Lazarro Hundt, PHA/CPH. By Ch. Maher's Top Gun V Hardt's ex Cullinane's Holly V Hardt's. Born 07/27/92. Bitch. *Judge:* Mrs. Marcia P. Tucker.
AKC Record: 30 Bests of Breed; 2 Group One placements.

The Great Dane combines, in its regal appearance, dignity, strength and elegance with great size and a powerful, well-formed, smoothly muscled body. It is one of the giant working breeds, but is unique in that its general conformation must be so well balanced that it never appears clumsy, and shall move with a long reach and powerful drive. It is always a unit—the Apollo of dogs. A Great Dane must be spirited, courageous, never timid or aggressive; always friendly and dependable. Dogs, ideally 32 inches or more; bitches, ideally 30 inches or more.

BEST OF OPPOSITE SEX:
Ch. Calico Rock Zuri V. Tiefburg. *Owners:* B. and D. Brown and C. and C. Abbott.
AWARDS OF MERIT:
Ch. Primrose Chase The Clouds. *Owner:* Mary Ellen Thomas.
Ch. V-Omega's Golden Treasure. *Owners:* Robert Conneen and Judith Lasardo.

GREAT PYRENEES
Am/Can/Mex/Int. Ch. Euzkalzale Sundance Legend

Breeders: Gene E. and Betty J. Beauchamp. *Owners:* Terry M. Denney-Combs and Karen Gieryk. *Handler:* Karen Gieryk. By Ch. Winterwood Asian On The Move ex Ch. Patou Lady Guinevere. Born 03/23/90. Dog. *Judge:* Mr. Burton J. Yamada.
AKC Record: 224 Bests of Breed; 24 Group One placements; 7 Bests in Show.

The Great Pyrenees dog conveys the distinct impression of elegance and unsurpassed beauty combined with great overall size and majesty. He possesses a keen intelligence and a kindly, while regal, expression. In nature, the Great Pyrenees is confident, gentle, and affectionate. While territorial and protective of his flock or family when necessary, his general demeanor is one of quiet composure, both patient and tolerant. He is strong willed, independent and somewhat reserved, yet attentive, fearless and loyal to his charges both human and animal. Dogs, 27 to 32 inches, 100 pounds and up; bitches, 25 to 29 inches, 85 pounds and up.

BEST OF OPPOSITE SEX:
    Ch. Chamrox Clarice. *Owner:* Maureen M. Walsh.
AWARDS OF MERIT:
    Ch. Pyrless Prime Time. *Owners:* Guy and Karen Justin and
        Valerie Seeley.
    Ch. Ville Vieux Mcroi Of Killaloe. *Owner:* Nora McDonald.

GREATER SWISS MOUNTAIN DOG

Ch. Derby Darling Belline

Breeder: Kristen M. Kleeman. *Owners:* Dr. and Mrs. John Allen and Kristen Kleeman. *Handler:* James A. Moses. By Ch. Sudbach's Guiness Xtra Stout ex Shadetree Aurora SeaVaRidge. Born 12/03/94. Bitch. *Judge:* Mrs. James Edward Clark.
AKC Record: 17 Bests of Breed.

The Greater Swiss Mountain Dog is a draft breed and should structurally appear as such. It is a striking, tri-colored, large, powerful dog of sturdy appearance. Bold, faithful, willing worker. Alert and vigilant. Dogs, 25 ½ to 28 ½ inches; bitches, 23 ½ to 27 inches.

BEST OF OPPOSITE SEX:
Ch. Jotunheim Finn McCoul. *Owners:* Joe and Cathy Donovan.
AWARDS OF MERIT:
Ch. Solsbury's Bergi Of Gfm. *Owner:* Mrs. Kim Busch.
Ch. Shamrock Leader. *Owners:* Karen and Skip Conant.

KOMONDOR

Ch. Lajosmegyi Far And Away

Breeders: John Landis, Barbara Artim and R. and E. Halmi. *Owners:* Anna Quigley, Patricia Turner and R. Halmi. By Ch. Lajosmegyi Dahu Digal ex Ch. Mogyorodi-Bundas Bodza. Born 03/09/92. Dog. *Judge:* Mrs. Lynette J. Saltzman.
AKC Record: 29 Bests of Breed; 3 Group One placements; 1 Best in Show.

The Komondor is characterized by imposing strength, courageous demeanor, and pleasing conformation. An excellent houseguard. It is wary of strangers. As a guardian of herds, it is, when grown, an earnest, courageous, and very faithful dog. It is devoted to its master and will defend him against attack by any stranger. Because of this trait, it is not used for driving the herds, but only for guarding them. The Komondor's special task is to protect the animals. It lives during the greater part of the year in the open, without protection against strange dogs and beasts of prey.
Dogs, 25½ inches; bitches, 23½ inches.

BEST OF OPPOSITE SEX:
Ch. Cabin Creek Poison Ivy. *Owners:* Richard and Therese Heaney.

KUVASZ
Ch. Szumeria's Sumer Solo

Breeders: Lynn Brady, C.D. Townsend and C. Hoffman. *Owners:* Lynn Brady, C.D. Townsend and C. Hoffman. *Handler:* James A. Moses. By Ch. Nordland's Rocky ex Ch. Oak Hill's Inanna Of Sumar. Born 09/28/94. Bitch. *Judge:* Mrs. Lynette J. Saltzman.
AKC Record: 48 Bests of Breed; 2 Group One placements.

The Kuvasz impresses the eye with strength and activity combined with light-footedness, moving freely on strong legs. A spirited dog of keen intelligence, determination, courage and curiosity. Very sensitive to praise and blame. Primarily a one-family dog. Devoted, gentle and patient with being overly demonstrative. Extremely strong instinct to protect children. Polite to accepted strangers, but rather suspicious and very discriminating in making new friends. Unexcelled guard, possessing ability to act on his own initiative at just the right moment without instruction. Bold, courageous and fearless. Dogs, 28 to 30 inches, 100 to 115 pounds; bitches, 26 to 28 inches, 70 to 90 pounds.

BEST OF OPPOSITE SEX:
Ch. Szumeria's Sargon Of Sumer. *Owners:* L. Brady C. Hoffman and C. Townsend.

MASTIFF
Ch. Iron Hills Into The Night

Breeder: Scott Phoebus. *Owners:* Glenn and Mary Capelle. By Ch. Iron Hills Paint Your Wagon ex Kara Stonehage. Born 07/06/93. Dog. *Judge:* Mrs. James Edward Clark.
AKC Record: 44 Bests of Breed; 5 Group One placements; 1 Best in Show.

The Mastiff is a large, massive, symmetrical dog with a well-knit frame. A combination of grandeur and good nature, courage and docility. Dignity, rather than gaiety, is the Mastiff's correct demeanor. Dogs, minimum 30 inches; bitches, minimum 27½ inches.

BEST OF OPPOSITE SEX:
Ch. Semper Fi Truly Impressive. *Owner:* Maggi Aherns.
AWARDS OF MERIT:
Ch. Bowsprit Bar's Song of the Sea. *Owners:* Kim Ward and Robert Bacso.
Ch. Creekside NKOTB Mighty Hogan. *Owners:* Mary Ann Keirnans and Eva Gomez.
Ch. Semper Fi Groppetti Gargoyle. *Owners:* P.J. Warfield and S. Owens.
Ch. Ridgewoods Otis. *Owners:* Carla and Joe Sanchez.

NEWFOUNDLAND
Ch. Steamboat's Highland Piper

Breeder: Elizabeth J. Stackhouse. *Owner:* Ann E. Sorm. *Handler:* Michael Floyd. By Ch. Topmast's John Huston ex Ch. Steamboat's Abagail Adams, CD. Born 06/28/92. Dog. *Judge:* Mrs. James Edward Clark. *AKC Record:* 79 Bests of Breed; 14 Group One placements; 4 Bests in Show.

The Newfoundland is a sweet-dispositioned dog that acts neither dull nor ill-tempered. He is a devoted companion. A multi-purpose dog, at home on land and in water, the Newfoundland is capable of draft work and possesses natural lifesaving ability. A good specimen of the breed has dignity and proud head carriage. Sweetness of temperament is the hallmark of the Newfoundland; this is the most important single characteristic of the breed. Dogs, 28 inches, 130 to 150 pounds; bitches, 26 inches, 100 to 120 pounds.

BEST OF OPPOSITE SEX:
Ch. Kiredor Masquerade Clough PND. *Owners:* Stacy and Linda Roderick.
AWARDS OF MERIT:
Ch. Schwartzbarhof's Walter Mitty. *Owners:* Robert Ramig and C. Derench.
Ch. Tabu's Don Juan Of Seabrook. *Owners:* Suzanne Atten, Mike Sterns and L. Lomax.
Ch. Pouch Cove's Britannia Rico. *Owners:* Reegan and Steven Keeler.

PORTUGUESE WATER DOG
Ch. Nautique's Noite De Casalago

Breeder: Linda M. Fowler. *Owners:* Tim O'Neill, R. Kweder, and R. Fowler. *Handlers:* Bobby Schoenfeld and Kay Palade. By Ch. Farmion Helmsman, CD ex Ch. Aquaries Blythe Spirit. Born 04/18/94. Bitch. *Judge:* Mrs. Lynete J. Saltzman.
AKC Record: 100 Bests of Breed; 3 Group One placements.

Known for centuries along Portugal's coast, this seafaring breed was prized by fishermen for a spirited, yet obedient nature, and a robust, medium build that allowed for a full day's work in and out of the water. The Portuguese Water Dog is a swimmer and diver of exceptional ability and stamina, who aided his master at sea by retrieving broken nets, herding schools of fish, and carrying messages between boats and to shore. An animal of spirited disposition, self-willed, brave, and very resistant to fatigue. A dog of exceptional intelligence and a loyal companion, it obeys its master with facility and apparent pleasure. Dogs, 20 to 23 inches, 42 to 60 pounds; bitches, 17 to 21 inches, 35 to 50 pounds.

BEST OF OPPOSITE SEX:
Ch. Pine Havens Had To Be You. *Owner:* Sally Griffith.
AWARDS OF MERIT:
Ch. Querida's Brigao. *Owner:* Cynthia O'Connor.
Ch. Carousel Fayre Britomart. *Owner:* Dorothy Rouse-Bottom.
Ch. Dacher's Monsoon. *Owners:* David E. and Sheryl Smith.

ROTTWEILER
Ch. Champ Vom Vilstaler Land

Breeder: Michael Stuckenberger. *Owners:* Evie and Manson Johnson and Julian and Adrian Burns. *Handler:* Bert N. Halsey. By Ch. Doc Von Der Teufelsbrucke ex Ubrina Vom Haus Winter. Born 11/10/91. Dog. *Judge:* Mr. Josef Hedi.
AKC Record: 17 Bests of Breed.

The Rottweiler is basically a calm, confident and courageous dog with a self assured aloofness that does not lend itself to immediate and indiscriminate friendships. A Rottweiler is self-confident and responds quietly and with a wait-and-see attitude to influences in his environment. He has an inherent desire to protect home and family, and is an intelligent dog of extreme hardness and adaptability with a strong willingness to work, making him especially suited as a companion, guardian and general all-purpose dog. Dogs, 24 to 27 inches; bitches, 22 to 25 inches.

BEST OF OPPOSITE SEX:
  Ch. Double D Maitai. *Owner:* Debbie Coon.
AWARDS OF MERIT:
  Ch. Roeckner's Ayla Cade. *Owners:* Teresa L. Osborn and Brenda L. Jayne.
  Ch. Napoleon Wolfgang Armadius CD. *Owner:* Manuel Burgo.
  Ch. Indian Ridge's Apache V Epic. *Owners:* D. Guthro and R. Carner.
  Ch. Gamegards Moonraker. *Owner:* Ellen B. Walls.
  Ch. Janesa's Mein Madchen. *Owner:* Heath Collier.

SAINT BERNARD
Ch. Lynchcreek's Executive

Breeders: Candace Blancher and Penny P. Mahon. *Owners:* Catherine and Clyde E. Dunphy, DVM. By Ch. Stoan's Knute Of Jaz ex Ch. Stoan's Ginny Mae O'Lynchcreek. Born 05/28/91. Dog. *Judge:* Mrs. James Edward Clark.
AKC Record: 155 Bests of Breed, including Westminster Kennel Club 1994; 31 Group One placements; 6 Bests in Show.

Powerful, proportionately tall figure, strong and muscular in every part, with powerful head and most intelligent expression.
He is gentle, friendly and easygoing, always acting in a noble manner, Saints can adapt to indoor or outdoor living and need a moderate amount of daily exercise. Dogs, 27½ inches minimum; bitches, 25 inches.

BEST OF OPPOSITE SEX:
Ch. Opdyke's Talk The Talk. *Owners:* Carol Vanderhoof and Glenn Radcliffe.
AWARDS OF MERIT:
Ch. Lil Jon's Brando Colone Wood. *Owners:* Robert C. Wood and Eva L. Colone.
Ch. Almshaus Double The Pleasure. *Owner:* Elizabeth Surface.

SAMOYED

Ch. Hoof'n Paws A Rose Is A Rose

Breeder: Mardee Ward. *Owners:* Mardee and Dolly Ward and Jeff and Nan Bennett. *Handler:* Robert M. Chaffin. By Ch. Hoof'n Paws Knight Shadow ex Ch. Hoof'n Paws Ramblin' Rose. Born 03/12/93. Bitch. *Judge:* Mrs. Lynette J. Saltzman.
AKC Record: 117 Bests of Breed; 18 Group One placements.

The Samoyed, being essentially a working dog, should present the picture of beauty, alertness and strength, with agility, dignity and grace. Intelligent, gentle, loyal, adaptable, alert, full of action, eager to serve, friendly but conservative, not distrustful or shy, not overly aggressive. Dogs, 21 to 23½ inches; bitches, 19 to 21 inches.

BEST OF OPPOSITE SEX:
    Ch. Whitecliff's Ted Sattu Karu. *Owners:* Carol Snow and Frances Powers.
AWARDS OF MERIT:
    Ch. Winterfrost's Gyrflcon. *Owner:* Louise J. O'Connell.
    Ch. Karu's Albert E Bykhal. *Owners:* Frances Powers and Bonnie Giffin.
    Ch. Samtara Striking Reflection. *Owners:* Kathleen F. and Steven F. Kersten.

SIBERIAN HUSKY
Am/Can. Ch. Tullemore's All In The Family

Breeders: Mary and Phil Norris. *Owners:* Linn and William Schleizer and Jacquie Wunder. *Handler:* Mike Szabo, CPH/DHG. By Ch. Tullemore In the Spotlite ex Ch. Tullemore's Keepsake. Born 01/16/92. Dog. *Judge:* Mrs. Marcia P. Tucker.
AKC Record: 94 Bests of Breed; 6 Group One placements; 1 Best in Show.

The Siberian Husky is a medium-size working dog, quick and light on his feet and free and graceful in action. He performs his function in harness most capably, carrying a light load at a moderate speed over great distances. The characteristic temperament of the Siberian Husky is friendly and gentle, but also alert and outgoing. He does not display the possessive qualities of the guard dog, nor is he overly suspicious of strangers or aggressive with other dogs. Some measure of reserve and dignity may be expected in the mature dog. His intelligence, tractability, and eager disposition make him an agreeable companion and willing worker. Dogs, 21 to 23½ inches, 45 to 60 pounds; bitches, 20 to 22 inches, 35 to 50 pounds.

BEST OF OPPOSITE SEX:
   Ch. Innisfree's Kiss 'N Tell. *Owner:* Maryann Simmons.
AWARDS OF MERIT:
   Ch. Innisfree's Ice-T. *Owners:* Kathleen Kanzer and M. Seki.
   Ch. Solocha's Magnum PI. *Owners:* Tyra Hunt and Betty Charlton.
   Ch. Kontoki's Uh-Huh! *Owners:* Thos Oelschlager, Marlene DePalma and A. and A. Amaral.

STANDARD SCHNAUZER

Ch. Parsifal Di Casa Netzer

Breeder: Gabrio Del Torre. *Owners:* Gabrio Del Torre and Rita Holloway. *Handler:* Douglas R. Holloway, Jr. By Jan Dum Torre ex Nina Del Torre. Born 04/14/91. Dog. *Judge:* Mr. Burton J. Yamada.
AKC Record: 357 Bests of Breed; 152 Group One placements; 65 Bests in Show.

GROUP 1

The Standard Schnauzer is a robust, heavy-set dog, sturdily built with good muscle and plenty of bone; square-built in proportion of body length to height. The Standard Schnauzer has highly developed senses, intelligence, aptitude for training, fearlessness, endurance and resistance against weather and illness. His nature combines high-spirited temperament with extreme reliability. Dogs, 18½ to 19½ inches; bitches, 17½ to 18½ inches.

BEST OF OPPOSITE SEX:
Ch. Flamme's Fire Brand. *Owners:* Alice Sesler and Helena Wask.
AWARD OF MERIT:
Ch. Von Schatten's Rave Review. *Owners:* Leona E. and Roslyn Mintz.

TERRIER DOGS

From the Latin word *terra* (earth) comes our word "terrier" describing dogs with stamina, unwavering determination, and courage to go to ground after their game.

The Terriers vary in size and form; bred to route out and kill vermin such as foxes, weasels, and rats, they have been crossed with mastiff breeds to produce hunters and guard dogs with terrier aggressiveness, courage and determination, as well as unmatched loyalty and devotion to their owners.

There are 26 breeds or varieties in the Terrier Group:

Airedale Terrier
American Staffordshire Terrier
Australian Terrier
Bedlington Terrier
Border Terrier
Bull Terrier (Colored)
Bull Terrier (White)
Cairn Terrier
Dandie Dinmont Terrier
Fox Terrier (Smooth)
Fox Terrier (Wire)
Irish Terrier
Kerry Blue Terrier
Lakeland Terrier
Manchester Terrier (Standard)
Miniature Bull Terrier
Miniature Schnauzer
Norfolk Terrier
Norwich Terrier
Scottish Terrier
Sealyham Terrier
Skye Terrier
Soft Coated Wheaten Terrier
Staffordshire Bull Terrier
Welsh Terrier
West Highland White Terrier

AIREDALE TERRIER
Ch. Tartan Scottshire Cowboy

Breeder: E. Forbes Gordon. *Owners:* Carol Greenwald and Carol L. Scott. *Handler:* Connie Clark. By Finlair Scottshire Maui Kris ex Ch. Tartan's Fancy Miss. Born 08/18/91. Dog. *Judge:* Mrs. Anne S. Katona. *AKC Record:* 96 Bests of Breed; 11 Group One placements; 1 Best in Show.

The Airedale Terrier is an elegant but sturdy dog, well balanced and square with the height at the withers being the same as the length from shoulder point to buttock—appearing neither short in the front legs nor high in the rear. None of the dog's features is exaggerated—the general impression is one of moderation and balance. The expression is eager and intelligent, and the Airedale appears self-confident, unafraid of people or other dogs. Airedales are more reserved in temperament than many of the other breeds, but should not act in a shy manner when approached by strangers. Dogs, approximately 23 inches; bitches, slightly less.

BEST OF OPPOSITE SEX:
   Ch. Tartan-Scottshire Kristina. *Owners:* William A. and Joan M. Clarke.
AWARDS OF MERIT:
   Ch. Epoch's Midnight Hour. *Owners:* Douglas and Aletta Moore.
   Ch. Serendipity Eagle's Wings. *Owners:* Mr. Joesph A. Vaudo and
      Barbara Schneider

AMERICAN STAFFORDSHIRE TERRIER

Ch. Fraja E.C. Young Rider

Breeders: John C. McCartney and Kimberly A. Roberts. *Owners:* Yunhee and Kihong Kim. *Handler:* Douglas R. Holloway, Jr. By Ch. Fraja E.C. Ruff Rider ex Ch. Fraja E.C. Shadow Chaser. Born 10/18/91. Dog. *Judge:* Mrs. Sandra Goose Allen.
AKC Record: 250 Bests of Breed, including Westminster Kennel Club 1994 and 1995; 36 Group One placements; 1 Best in Show.

The American Staffordshire Terrier should give the impression of great strength for his size, a well-put-together dog, muscular, but agile and graceful, keenly alive to his surroundings. He should be stocky, not long-legged or racy in outline. His courage is proverbial. Dogs, 18 to 19 inches; bitches, 17 to 18 inches.

BEST OF OPPOSITE SEX:
Ch. Wolfs Louisiana Purchase. *Owner:* Stephen Chisolm and Carolyn B. Wolfe.
AWARDS OF MERIT:
Ch. Cloverhill's Dance Across Texas. *Owner:* Maureen Harriman.
Ch. Benmars Sharp Shooter. *Owners:* John Willet, Lucille Walters and Marcela Cheek.
Ch. Sierra-Gaff Titanium Tank. *Owner:* Lorene Wilson.
Ch. Benmar's Macho Of Roadhouse. *Owners:* J. and G. Wragg, G. Roadhouse and B. Cheek.

AUSTRALIAN TERRIER
Ch. Eager April Thunder

Breeder: Gertrude E. Reida. *Owners:* Nell N. Fox and Diane Roy. *Handler:* Peter J. Green. By Ch. Brandywine's Big Bam Boom ex Ch. Eager Mischievous Maureen. Born 04/18/92. Dog. *Judge:* Mrs. Anne S. Katona.
AKC Record: 125 Bests of Breed; 2 Group One placements.

A small, sturdy, medium-boned working terrier. As befits their heritage as versatile workers, Australian Terriers are sound and free moving with good reach and drive. Their expression keen and intelligent; their manner spirited and self-assured. The Australian Terrier is spirited, alert, courageous, and self-confident, with the natural aggressiveness of a ratter and hedge hunter; as a companion, friendly and affectionate. Dogs and bitches, 10 to 11 inches.

BEST OF OPPOSITE SEX:
   Ch. Bearstep's Uluru Rocka Tekoah. *Owners:* Dave and Debbie Hempstead.
AWARD OF MERIT:
   Ch. Yaralla's Rock The Ring. *Owner:* Eva Steele.

BEDLINGTON TERRIER

Ch. Willow Wind Money Talks

Breeder: David Ramsey. *Owners:* David Ramsey and Kerry Himmelberger. *Handler:* David Ramsey. By Ch. Willow Wind Play It My Way ex Ch. Willow Wind Memory Lane. Born 03/27/94. Dog. *Judge:* Mrs. Anne S. Katona.
AKC Record: 192 Bests of Breed, including Westminster Kennel Club 1996; 83 Group One placements; 21 Bests in Show.

A graceful, lithe, well-balanced dog with no sign of coarseness, weakness or shelliness. In repose the expression is mild and gentle, not shy or nervous. Aroused, the dog is particularly alert and full of immense energy and courage. Noteworthy for endurance, Bedlingtons also gallop at great speed, as their body outline clearly shows. Dogs, 16½ inches; bitches, 15½ inches.

GROUP 2

BEST OF OPPOSITE SEX:
Ch. Carillon Serendipity Citrine. *Owners:* Lucy Heyman and Jan Nichols.
AWARD OF MERIT:
Ch. Willow Wind It's My Party. *Owner:* Jacquelyn Fogel.

BORDER TERRIER
Ch. Krispin Tailored To A T

Breeder: Dail P. Corl. *Owners:* Betsy Kirkpatrick, Cindy Peebles and W. Henry Odum III. *Handler:* Michael E. Scott. By Ch. Krispin Tailor Made ex Ch. Krispin Wuzzle. Born 03/01/92. Dog. *Judge:* Mrs. Anne S. Katona. *AKC Record:* 191 Bests of Breed, including Westminster Kennel Club 1995; 34 Group One placements; 5 Bests in Show.

He is an active terrier of medium bone, strongly put together, suggesting endurance and agility. Since the Border Terrier is a working terrier of a size to go to ground and able, within reason, to follow a horse, his conformation should be such that he be ideally built to do his job. For this work he must be alert, active and agile, and capable of squeezing through narrow apertures and rapidly traversing any kind of terrain. By nature he is good-tempered, affectionate, obedient and easily trained. In the field he is hard as nails, "game as they come" and driving in attack. Dogs, 13 to 15½ pounds; bitches, 11½ to 14 pounds.

BEST OF OPPOSITE SEX:
    Ch. CB's Dreidel. *Owner:* Bonnie Rosenberg.
AWARDS OF MERIT:
    Ch. Krispins Smart Alec. *Owners:* Gary and Paula Wolf.
    Ch. Calirose Prize Patrol JE. *Owners:* Lisa Connelly, Charles Vance and
        Helen Vance.
    Ch. Standish's A Dream Come True. *Owners:* J. Standish, R. Maxwell
        and J. Strassels.

BULL TERRIER (COLORED)

Ch. Action Hot Tomato

Breeders: Franne Berez, MD and Maureen C. Siwiec. *Owners:* Leslie Lehmann, Bruce Dunlap, MD and Franne Berez, MD. *Handler:* Leslie Lehmann. By Bullyview Rytham Dancer ex Ch. Action Hot Item. Born 05/10/95. Bitch. *Judge:* Dr. Robert J. Berndt.
AKC Record: 3 Bests of Breed.

The Bull Terrier must be strongly built, muscular, symmetrical and active, with a keen determined and intelligent expression, full of fire but of sweet disposition and amenable to discipline. Bull Terriers usually exhibit a degree of animation and individuality in the ring. They should not be penalized for their exuberant approach if they are not overly disruptive or aggressive. Bull Terriers live nicely with other animals and are trustworthy with children.

BEST OF OPPOSITE SEX:
Ch. Windfall's Windcatcher. *Owner:* Gay Hillman.
AWARD OF MERIT:
Ch. Coronado's Wild Dusty Rose. *Owners:* Terry E. and Regina G. May.

BULL TERRIER (WHITE)

Ch. Iceni Incantation

Breeders: Robert and Lynne Myall and Pamela Maalea. *Owners:* Robert and Lynne Myall. By Jebt's Royal Reagh At Iceni ex Ch. Iceni Sweet Mischief Maker. Born 03/26/94. Bitch. *Judge:* Dr. Robert J. Berndt. *AKC Record:* 12 Bests of Breed.

The Bull Terrier must be strongly built, muscular, symmetrical and active, with a keen determined and intelligent expression, full of fire but of sweet disposition and amenable to discipline. Bull Terriers usually exhibit a degree of animation and individuality in the ring. They should not be penalized for their exuberant approach if they are not overly disruptive or aggressive. Bull Terriers live nicely with other animals and are trustworthy with children.

BEST OF OPPOSITE SEX:
Ch. Birnamwood's Hot Action. *Owners:* Leslie Lehmann, Bruce Dunlap MD, and Maureen Siwiec.

CAIRN TERRIER
Ch. Copperglen Windwalker

Breeder: Carol J. Ackerson. *Owners:* Marianne and William J. Ham. *Handlers:* Bergit Coady and Greg Strong. By Ch. Sharolaine's Kalypso ex Ch. Copperglen Fame and Fortune. Born 05/21/91 Dog. *Judge:* Dr. Robert J. Berndt.
AKC Record: 80 Bests of Breed; 1 Group One placement.

An active, game, hardy, small working terrier of short-legged class. Dogs, 10 inches, 14 pounds; bitches, 9½ inches, 13 pounds. No two Cairns are truly alike: each has distinct personality. As a rule, though, Cairns are somewhat independent. Their intelligence makes them curious and extremely quick to learn. They are surprisingly sensitive, and harsh punishment is not necessary or desirable. Cairns seem to have an in-born affinity for children. Cairns are not suited to living outside. They are far more rewarding pets when they live in close contact with their family.

BEST OF OPPOSITE SEX:
Ch. Meadowwyn's One Trick Pony. *Owners:* Frank Mesich and Glenn Sergius.
AWARDS OF MERIT:
Ch. Cook's Misty Meadow D-Day. *Owner:* Marcella Cobb.
Ch. Grace Of Lucky Karma. *Owner:* KiKuKo Ohara.

DANDIE DINMONT TERRIER

Ch. Loughran's Lamborghini

Breeder: Mrs. Edward Ozorowski. *Owners:* David Ruml and I.F. Zimmerman. *Handler:* Geoff Browne. By Ch. Dunsandle Partridge Macpence ex Ch. Munchkintown's Lisa Marie. Born 09/29/93. Dog. *Judge:* Mrs. Sandra Goose Allen.
AKC Record: 159 Bests of Breed; 2 Group One placements.

Originally bred to go to ground, the Dandie Dinmont Terrier is a long, low-stationed working terrier with a curved outline. Independent, determined, reserved and intelligent. The Dandie Dinmont Terrier combines an affectionate and dignified nature with, in a working situation, tenacity and boldness. Dogs and bitches, 8 to 11 inches, 18 to 24 pounds.

BEST OF OPPOSITE SEX:
Ch. Katiedid's Ms. Liberty Belle. *Owner:* Carol R. Hamilton.

FOX TERRIER (SMOOTH)

Ch. Warfox Steeplechase

Breeders: M.S. Nelson and Jan Smith. *Owner:* M.S. Nelson. *Handler:* Elizabeth Tobin. By Ch. Laurelton Now or Never ex Ch. The Winds Of Warfox Jrees. Born 06/10/95. Dog. *Judge:* Mrs. Sandra Goose Allen. *AKC Record:* 25 Bests of Breed; 1 Group One placement; 1 Best in Show.

The dog must present a generally gay, lively and active appearance. He should stand like a cleverly made hunter, covering a lot of ground, yet with a short back. Dogs, not exceeding 15½ inches; bitches, proportionally less.

BEST OF OPPOSITE SEX:
  Ch. Quissex Radwyn Gold Lace. *Owner:* Mrs. M.E. McLean.
AWARDS OF MERIT:
  Ch. Buckleigh Dressed To Kill. *Owners:* Mr. and Mrs. Michael D. Buckley and Sergio Balcazar.
  Ch. Son-Es El Ojo Negro Teller. *Owner:* Sergio Balcazar.

FOX TERRIER (WIRE)

Ch. Random Reaction

Breeders: W. James and Taffe McFadden. *Owners:* W. James and Taffe McFadden. *Handler:* Bill McFadden. By Ch. Blazencrest After Hours ex Random Right On Maxine. Born 08/27/94. Dog. *Judge:* Mrs. Sandra Goose Allen.
AKC Record: 2 Bests of Breed.

The dog must present a generally gay, lively and active appearance. He should stand like a cleverly made hunter, covering a lot of ground, yet with a short back. Dogs, not exceeding 15½ inches; bitches, proportionally less.

GROUP 1

BEST OF OPPOSITE SEX:
    Ch. Foxhollow Ain't Misbehaven. *Owner:* Susan M. Carter.
AWARDS OF MERIT:
    Ch. Brookhaven Go For Broke. *Owners:* Kathleen Reges and Mari M.
        Morissey.
    Ch. Sir John Du Bois Des Maitres. *Owners:* Mr. and Mrs. J. Felix, R.
        Chashoudian and K. Reges.

KERRY BLUE TERRIER

Ch. Dame Jane BTM Of The Jean

Breeder: Mrs. Jean B. Underhill. *Owner:* Mrs. Jean B. Underhill. *Handler:* Douglas R. Holloway, Jr. By Ch. Travelling Man V Dalenbroek ex Ch. Bonnie J.L. Of The Jean. Born 05/06/93. Bitch. *Judge:* Mrs. Anne S. Katona.
AKC Record: 80 Bests of Breed.

The typical Kerry Blue Terrier should be upstanding, well knit and in good balance, showing a well developed and muscular body with definite terrier style and character throughout. The Kerry Blue makes an ideal house pet. A natural hunter, a born retriever and a fine herd dog—he is used for these purposes in the old country. He is not a yapper, and seldom barks. A Kerry Blue remains playful...a real companion...years longer than most breeds. Dogs, 18 to 19½ inches; bitches, 17½ to 19 inches.

BEST OF OPPOSITE SEX:
Ch. Melbee's Double Jeopardy. *Owner:* Melbee Kennels.
AWARDS OF MERIT:
Ch. Goodspice Shayna Punam. *Owner:* Irving Moskowitz.
Ch. Fellbrin's I'm A Holy Tara Too. *Owners:* Fern R. and Fred W. Rogers.

LAKELAND TERRIER

Ch. Revelry's Awesome Blossom

Breeder: Dawn M. Markham. *Owners:* Jean L. Heath and William H. Cosby Jr. *Handler:* Clay Coady. By Ch. Black Watch Moonshine ex. Ch. Black Watch Briarrose. Born 04/09/93. Bitch. *Judge:* Dr. Robert J. Berndt. *AKC Record:* 261 Bests of Breed, including Westminster Kennel Club 1995; 189 Group One placements; 82 Bests in Show.

The Lakeland Terrier was bred to hunt vermin in the rugged shale mountains of the Lake District of northern England. He is a small, workmanlike dog of square, sturdy build. The typical Lakeland Terrier is bold, gay and friendly, with a confident, cock-of-the-walk attitude. Shyness, especially shysharpness, in the mature specimen, and aggressiveness are to be strongly discouraged. Dogs, 14½ inches, 17 pounds; bitches, 13½ inches.

GROUP 4

AWARD OF MERIT:
Ch. Aurahil Heartlight V Sujawe. *Owners:* Don and Edna Lawicki and D. and E. Lawler.

MANCHESTER TERRIER (STANDARD)
Ch. Oasis Warbonnet

Breeders: James and Janice Wetton and Gary and Judy Anderson. *Owner:* I. Cary. *Handler:* Richard Plaut.
By Ch. Oasis Dickens Of Anozira ex Ch. Oasis Emma Page Of Anozira. Born 03/01/95. Dog. *Judge:* Dr.
Robert J. Berndt.
AKC Record: 37 Bests of Breed.

The Manchester Terrier is neither aggressive nor shy. He is keenly observant, devoted, but discerning. Not being a sparring breed, the Manchester is generally friendly with other dogs. Dogs and bitches, over 12 but not exceeding 22 pounds.

BEST OF OPPOSITE SEX:
Ch. Salutaire No Foolin. *Owners:* Barbara Odell and Myrtle Klensch.
AWARD OF MERIT:
Ch. Neverland's Moody Blue CD. *Owners:* Stuart and Roberta L. Berman.

MINIATURE BULL TERRIER

Ch. Stainsby Soup Of The Day

Breeders: Mr. L. and Mrs. S.A. Lonsdale. *Owners:* L. Holland, Dana Cline and B. Wycoff. *Handler:* Dana Cline.
By Badlesmere Bertie Wooster ex Ch. Eiraght X-Rated At Stainsby. Born 12/31/93. Dog. *Judge:* Dr. Robert
J. Berndt.
AKC Record: 37 Bests of Breed; 1 Group One placement.

The Miniature Bull Terrier must be strongly built, symmetrical and active, with a
keen, determined and intelligent ex-
pression. He should be full of fire,
having a courageous, even temperament and be amenable to discipline.
Dogs and bitches, 10 to 14 inches.

BEST OF OPPOSITE SEX:
    Ch. Crescent Nefertari. *Owner:* Susan Hall, DVM.
AWARD OF MERIT:
    Ch. Crescent Symmetry. *Owner:* Richard Ciecwisz.

MINIATURE SCHNAUZER

Ch. Nicknack Love On The Run

Breeder: Carla C. Nickerson. *Owners:* Martin and Margo Dettelbach. *Handler:* Carla C. Nickerson. By Ch. Adamis Frontrunner ex Ch. Nicknack Partner In Crime. Born 10/26/95. Bitch. *Judge:* Dr. Robert J. Berndt. *AKC Record:* 3 Bests of Breed; 1 Group One placement.

The Miniature Schnauzer is a robust, active dog of terrier type, resembling his larger cousin, the Standard Schnauzer, in general appearance and of an alert, active disposition. The typical Miniature Schnauzer is alert and spirited, yet obedient to command. He is friendly, intelligent and willing to please. He should never be overaggressive or timid. Dogs and bitches, 12 to 14 inches.

BEST OF OPPOSITE SEX:
Ch. Ruedesheim's Financier. *Owner:* Anne D. Lockney.
AWARD OF MERIT:
Ch. Adamis Annie Oakley. *Owner:* Carla Nickerson.

NORFOLK TERRIER

Ch. Max-Well's Weatherman

Breeder: Mrs. Barbara Miller. *Owner:* Mrs. Barbara Miller. *Handler:* Susan Kipp. By Ch. Nanfan Culver ex Ch. Max-Well's Whizard Of Oz. Born 12/12/92. Dog. *Judge:* Mrs. Barbara S. Fournier.
AKC Record: 179 Bests of Breed, including Westminster Kennel Club 1996; 72 Group One placements; 12 Bests in Show.

The Norfolk Terrier, game and hardy, with expressive dropped ears, is one of the smallest of the working terriers. It is active and compact, free-moving, with good substance and bone. With its natural, weather-resistant coat and short legs, it is a "perfect demon" in the field. This versatile, agreeable breed can go to ground, bolt a fox and tackle or dispatch other small vermin, working alone or with a pack. In temperament, alert, gregarious, fearless and loyal. Never aggressive. Dogs, 9 to 10 inches; bitches tend to be smaller.

GROUP 3

BEST OF OPPOSITE SEX:
Ch. Dakota's Fiddle Dee Dee. *Owners:* Sal Garofalo and Joan Rawlins.
AWARD OF MERIT:
Ch. Max-Well's Spring Into Action. *Owners:* Pamela and John F. Beale and Barbara Miller.

NORWICH TERRIER

Ch. Chestnut Hills Royal Blue

Breeders: Karen and Ron Anderson. *Owner:* Anna Bellenger. *Handler:* Margery Good. By Ch. Devondale's Master Milestone ex Chestnut Hills Trivet. Born 11/29/94. Dog. *Judge:* Mrs. Barbara S. Fournier. *AKC Record:* 5 Bests of Breed.

The Norwich Terrier, spirited and stocky with sensitive prick ears and a slightly foxy expression, is one of the smallest working terriers. This sturdy descendent of ratting companions, eager to dispatch small vermin alone or in a pack, has good bone and substance and an almost weatherproof coat. A hardy hunt terrier. In temperament, gay, fearless, loyal and affectionate. Adaptable and sporting, they make ideal companions. Dogs and bitches, not exceeding 10 inches, approximately 12 pounds.

BEST OF OPPOSITE SEX:
   Ch. Dunbar's Jet Setter. *Owners:* Mrs. Joan Schurr Kefeli and Helen B. Gathier.
AWARDS OF MERIT:
   Ch. Jerusalem Artichoke. *Owner:* Dr. Phyllis E. Pullen, MD.
   Ch. Kristil's Royal Conqueror. *Owners:* Jacqueline McMurray and Susan Kipp.

SCOTTISH TERRIER

Ch. Anstamm Brookwood Joint Venture

Breeders: Fred and Patty Brooks and Anstamm Kennels. *Owners:* Fred and Patty Brooks and Anstamm Kennels. *Handler:* C.L. Eudy. By Ch. Amescots Lotta Talk ex Ch. Anstamm Low Commotion. Born 06/21/93. Dog. *Judge:* Dr. Robert J. Berndt.
AKC Record: 91 Bests of Breed; 24 Group One placements; 2 Bests in Show.

The face should wear a keen, sharp and active expression. Both head and tail should be carried well up. The dog should look very compact, well muscled and powerful, giving the impression of immense power in a small size. Dogs, 10 inches, 19 to 22 pounds; bitches, 10 inches, 18 to 21 pounds.

BEST OF OPPOSITE SEX:
    Ch. Friendship Hill Anchor Woman. *Owners:* Patricia M. and
        Thomas G. Gallatin.
AWARDS OF MERIT:
    Ch. Thistlepark Seas The Moment. *Owners:* James and Margo Park.
    Ch. Amescot Hakuna Matata. *Owner:* Lindsey LeClair.

SEALYHAM TERRIER
Ch. Tinter Tzarina

Breeders: Cheryl L. Jennings and Diane H. Orange. *Owners:* David Ruml and I.F. Zimmerman. *Handler:* Geoff Browne. By Whimsy Wise Guy ex Ch. Counseler Tintern Superb. Born 04/18/94. Bitch. *Judge:* Dr. Robert J. Berndt.
AKC Record: 154 Bests of Breed; 25 Group One placements; 3 Bests in Show.

The Sealyham should be the embodiment of power and determination, ever keen and alert, of extraordinary substance, yet free from clumsiness. Dogs and bitches, 10½ inches, 23 to 24 pounds.
The Sealyham today is chiefly a companion, but when given the opportunity makes a very good working terrier. He is very outgoing, friendly yet a good house watchdog whose big-dog bark discourages intruders. He is easily trained but more often than not will add his own personal touch to the exercise or trick being taught.

BEST OF OPPOSITE SEX:
    Ch. Polrose Political Party. *Owner:* Wes Jones.
AWARD OF MERIT:
    Ch. Goodspice Pinch O The Shoulder. *Owners:* Bruce C. Pilch and Margery Good.

SKYE TERRIER

Ch. Longwood Piper's Promise

Breeders: Wayne R. and Audrey L. Herman and Kathryn A. Walling. *Owner:* Wayne R. Herman. *Handler:* Sharon Cook. By Ch. Battlewood Black Tie Affair ex Ch. Battlewood Classy Lass. Born 05/09/94. Dog. *Judge:* Mrs. Sandra Goose Allen.
AKC Record: 34 Bests of Breed; 3 Group One placements.

The Skye Terrier is a dog of style, elegance and dignity: agile and strong with sturdy bone and hard muscle. Long, low and level—he is twice as long as he is high. In temperament, a typical working terrier capable of overtaking game and going to ground, displaying stamina, courage, strength and agility. Fearless, good-tempered, loyal and canny, he is friendly and gay with those he knows and reserved and cautious with strangers. Dogs, 10 inches; bitches, 9½ inches.

> **BEST OF OPPOSITE SEX:**
> Ch. Skyeview Wee Bonnibelle. *Owners:* Authur and Diana Holzer.

STAFFORDSHIRE BULL TERRIER

Ch. Bullseye Battle Hymn

Breeders: Zane Smith and M. Cabral. *Owner:* Zane Smith. *Handler:* Kimberly Roberts. By Ch. Red Adair Lucky Warrior Of Samtor ex Cresstock Zenobia. Born 04/14/94. Dog. *Judge:* Mrs. Barbara S. Fournier. *AKC Record:* 126 Bests of Breed; 9 Group One placements.

The Staffordshire Bull Terrier should be of great strength for its size and, although muscular, should be active and agile. From the past history of the Staffordshire Bull Terrier, the modern dog draws its character of indomitable courage, high intelligence, and tenacity. This, coupled with its affection for its friends, and children in particular, its off-duty quietness and trustworthy stability, makes it a foremost all-purpose dog. Dogs, 14 to 16 inches, 28 to 38 pounds; bitches, 14 to 16 inches, 24 to 34 pounds.

BEST OF OPPOSITE SEX:
Ch. Mirkwood Rivendell Anna. *Owner:* Mike Goldfarb.
AWARD OF MERIT:
Ch. Roust-A-Bout's Packin' Heat. *Owners:* Chris and Christa Jacksic.

WEST HIGHLAND WHITE TERRIER

Ch. Glengloamin's Rise 'N Shine

Breeders: Randell Dickerson and Bill Green. *Owners:* Dr. James and Elizabeth Boso and G. and G. Miller. *Handler:* Bergit Coady. By Ch. Holyrood's Hotspur O'Shelly Bay ex Ch. Glengloamin's Fancy Free. Born 09/14/92. Bitch. *Judge:* Mrs. Barbara S. Fournier.
AKC Record: 81 Bests of Breed; 5 Group One placements; 1 Best in Show.

The West Highland White Terrier is a small, game, well-balanced hardy looking terrier, exhibiting good showmanship, possessed with no small amount of self-esteem. Alert, gay, courageous and self-reliant, but friendly. Dogs, 11 inches; bitches, 10 inches.

BEST OF OPPOSITE SEX:
    Ch. Orions Mercury. *Owners:* Ida and Joe Keushgenian.
AWARDS OF MERIT:
    Ch. Sudoeste's Little Feat. *Owners:* Debra Keushgenian and Nancy Stalnaker.
    Ch. Camcrest Andsurely Trouble. *Owner:* Sandy Campbell.

TOY DOGS

Bred down to pocket size, Toy dogs are popular in city and suburban households. Their special quality is their diminutiveness which, when coupled with healthy bodies and happy temperaments, makes them ideally suited as the family pet.

They often resemble their larger cousins in miniature form: the Pomeranian, unmistakably a Nordic dog; the Papillon, a little spaniel; the Toy Poodle, a tiny replica of dogs once used as retrievers in the field.

There are 21 breeds or varieties in the Toy Group:

Affenpinscher
Brussels Griffon
Cavalier King Charles Spaniel
Chihuahua (Long Coat)
Chihuahua (Smooth Coat)
Chinese Crested
English Toy Spaniel (Blenheim and Prince Charles)
English Toy Spaniel (King Charles and Ruby)
Italian Greyhound
Japanese Chin
Maltese
Manchester Terrier (Toy)
Miniature Pinscher
Papillon
Pekingese
Pomeranian
Poodle (Toy)
Pug
Shih Tzu
Silky Terrier
Yorkshire Terrier

AFFENPINSCHER

Ch. Terian's Black Storm Rising

Breeders: Dr. and Mrs. Brian J. Shack. *Owners:* Dr. and Mrs. Brian J. Shack. *Handler:* Dr. Brian J. Shack. By Ch. Osgood Farm's Mighty Mouse ex Ch. Rosehill's Midnight Rose. Born 04/18/94. Dog. *Judge:* Mrs. Eleanor L. Rotman.
AKC Record: 89 Bests in Breed; 7 Group One placements; 1 Best in Show.

The Affenpinscher is a balanced, little wiry-haired terrier-like toy dog whose intelligence and demeanor make it a good house pet. Originating in Germany, where the name Affenpinscher means "monkey-like terrier," the breed was developed to rid the kitchens, granaries and stables of rodents. In France the breed is described as the *diablotin moustachu* or the moustached little devil. Both these names help to describe the appearance and attitude of this delightful breed. The general demeanor of the Affenpinscher is game, alert and inquisitive with great loyalty and affection toward its master and friends. The breed is generally quiet but can become vehemently excited when threatened or attacked and is fearless toward any aggressor. Dogs and bitches, 9 to 11½ inches.

BEST OF OPPOSITE SEX:
　Ch. Gerbraes Maid In Splendor. *Owner:* Beth Sweigart.
AWARDS OF MERIT:
　Ch. Hilane's Harpagon. *Owners:* Shirley C. Howard and Kathy and Jim Herman.
　Ch. Ceterra's Little Black Sambo. *Owners:* C. L. Eudy and Jacob R. Hunt.

BRUSSELS GRIFFON
Ch. Toobee's Rembrandt

Breeders: Lana and Nancy Brooks. *Owners:* Dr. Harold, Nancy, and Lana Brooks. *Handler:* Nancy Brooks. By Ch. Pamelot's Over The Top ex Ch. Toobee's Esse Cherutoch. Born 10/12/94. Dog. *Judge:* Mrs. Eleanor L. Rotman.
AKC Record: 41 Bests of Breed; 5 Group One placements; 1 Best in Show.

A toy dog, intelligent, alert, sturdy, with a thickset, short body, a smart carriage and set-up, attracting attention by an almost human expression. In temperament, the Brussels Griffon is intelligent, alert and sensitive. Full of self-importance. Dogs and bitches, 8 to 10 pounds.

BEST OF OPPOSITE SEX:
Ch. Rickshaw's Spin To Win. *Owners:* P. Hamann, K. Miyamoto and B. Yamasaki.
AWARD OF MERIT:
Ch. Donandru's Benjamin Bunny. *Owner:* Ruth Periera.

CAVALIER KING CHARLES SPANIEL

GROUP 4

Ch. Partridge Wood Laughing Misdemeanor

Breeder: Debra King. *Owner:* Cindy Lazzeroni. *Handler:* Cindy Lazzeroni. By Laughing Charisma ex Laughing Must Be Magic. Born 06/11/91. Bitch. Judge: Dr. Jacklyn E. Hungerland.
AKC Record: 29 Bests of Breed.

An active, graceful, well-balanced dog, very gay and free in action, fearless and sporting in character, yet at the same time gentle and affectionate. It is the typical gay temperament, combined with true elegance and "royal" appearance, which is of paramount importance in the breed. Dogs and bitches, 12 to 13 inches; 13 to 18 pounds.

BEST OF OPPOSITE SEX:
Ch. Ravenrush Gillespie. *Owners:* John D. Gammon and Robert A. Schroll.

AWARDS OF MERIT:
Ch. Corneel V H Lamslag. *Owner:* Janet York.
Ch. Flying Colors Dangerous At Radiant. *Owners:* Cathy Gish and Ann Ray Hutton.
Ch. Hilarny Larkin About. *Owners:* Les and Elaine Pinkowski.
Ch. Wye Rebound Of Rattlebridge. *Owners:* Meredith Johnson-Synder and Lemont M. Yoder.

CHIHUAHUA
(LONG COAT)
Ch. Dartan's Magic Onyx

Breeder: Darwin L. Delaney. *Owners:* Steven E. and Beverly L. Gall. *Handler:* Michael Work, DHG/PHA. By Ch. McCormick's Pe Pe Le Blue ex Ch. Dartan's The Wonder Of Magic. Born 01/24/93. Dog. Judge: Mrs. Eleanor L. Rotman.
AKC Record: 117 Bests of Breed; 3 Group One placements.

A graceful, alert, swift-moving little dog with saucy expression, compact, and with terrier-like qualities of temperament. Dogs and bitches, not to exceed 6 pounds.
American breeders have produced a diminutive dog that has few comparisons, even among other breeds, in size, symmetry, and conformation, as well as intelligence and alertness. Curiously, the Chihuahua is clannish, recognizing and preferring his own kind, and, as a rule, not liking dogs of other breeds.

BEST OF OPPOSITE SEX:
Ch. Ouachitah Bijou. *Owner:* Mrs. Keith Thomas.
AWARDS OF MERIT:
Ch. Mar-Rich's Minute Man-L. *Owner:* Mary Price.
Ch. Dea's Candi Caine. *Owners:* Deanna French and Lerae Bush.

CHIHUAHUA
(SMOOTH COAT)
Ch. Regnier's Wistle For Willy

Breeder: Patricia A. Regnier. *Owners:* Deanna French and Patricia Regnier. *Handler:* Jim Lehman. By Ch. Widogi Willibegood ex Regnier's Rosalita Marie. Born 05/07/94. Dog. *Judge:* Mrs. Eleanor L. Rotman. *AKC Record:* 60 Bests of Breed; 1 Group One placement.

A graceful, alert, swift-moving little dog with saucy expression, compact, and with terrier-like qualities of temperament. Dogs and bitches, not to exceed 6 pounds.
American breeders have produced a diminutive dog that has few comparisons, even among other breeds, in size, symmetry, and conformation, as well as intelligence and alertness. Curiously, the Chihuahua is clannish, recognizing and preferring his own kind, and, as a rule, not liking dogs of other breeds.

BEST OF OPPOSITE SEX:
    Ch. Mt View's One Tender Lady. *Owners:* Tom and Jeanne Cooke and oanne Iannone.
AWARDS OF MERIT:
    Ch. Ouachitah Masterpiece. *Owner:* Mrs. Keith Thomas.
    Ch. Dea's Great Walls Of China. *Owner:* Deanna French.

CHINESE CRESTED

Ch. Trubo's Barney Google Cadaran

Breeders: Jon W. Six and Carol Nouza. *Owners:* Tom and Jeanne Cooke and Joanne Iannone. By Ch. Taleeca Technology ex Cadaran's Ru Pawl Of Jon Six. Born 03/17/96. Dog. *Judge:* Mr. R. Stephen Shaw. *AKC Record:* 11 Bests of Breed.

A Toy dog, fine-boned, elegant and graceful. The distinct varieties are born in the same litter. The Hairless with hair only on the head, tail and feet and the Powderpuff, completely covered with hair. The breed serves as a loving companion, playful and entertaining. In temperament, gay and alert. Dogs and bitches, ideally 11 to 13 inches.

BEST OF OPPOSITE SEX:
Ch. Makara's Shining Star. *Owner:* Sandi Weigand.
AWARDS OF MERIT:
Ch. Whispering Lane Painted Pony. *Owner:* Jean Brown.
Ch. Bayshore Sol-Orr Hi-Tech. *Owners:* Dail Corl and J. Frank Baylis.

ENGLISH TOY SPANIEL
(BLENHEIM & PRINCE CHARLES)
Ch. Debonaire Double Jeopardy

Breeder: Deborah K. Bowman. *Owner:* Deborah K. Bowman. *Handler:* Deborah K. Bowman. By Ch. Dreamridge Dear Sir ex Ch. Dreamidge Dear Jessica. Born 01/21/90. Dog. *Judge:* Mr. R. Stephen Shaw. *AKC Record:* 168 Bests of Breed, including Westminster Kennel Club 1995; 29 Group One placements; 2 Bests in Show.

The English Toy Spaniel is a compact, cobby and essentially square toy dog possessed of a short-nosed, domed head, a merry and affectionate demeanor and a silky, flowing coat. His compact, sturdy body and charming temperament, together with his rounded head, lustrous dark eye, and well cushioned face, proclaim him a dog of distinction and character. The English Toy Spaniel is a bright and interested little dog, affectionate and willing to please. Dogs and bitches, 8 to 14 pounds.

AWARD OF MERIT:
Ch. Debonaire Don't Stop Now. *Owner:* Deborah K. Bowman.

ENGLISH TOY SPANIEL
(KING CHARLES AND RUBY)
Ch. Kis'n Knoble Michael

Breeders: Susan C. and John L. Kisielewski. *Owners:* Mark S. and Jacqueline Stempel. *Handler:* Mark S. Stempel. By Ch. Kis'n King O Road ex Kis'n Karry Me Back. Born 05/22/92. Dog. *Judge:* Mr. R. Stephen Shaw.
AKC Record: 16 Bests of Breed.

The English Toy Spaniel is a compact, cobby and essentially square toy dog possessed of a short-nosed, domed head, a merry and affectionate demeanor and a silky, flowing coat. His compact, sturdy body and charming temperament, together with his rounded head, lustrous dark eye, and well cushioned face, proclaim him a dog of distinction and character. The English Toy Spaniel is a bright and interested little dog, affectionate and willing to please. Dogs and bitches, 8 to 14 pounds.

AWARD OF MERIT:
Ch. Maramond Mojo. *Owner:* Martha Guimond.

ITALIAN GREYHOUND

Ch. Bobett's Windermere Sirius Style

Breeders: Andrea Parker and Barbara Fischer. *Owner:* Richardo Ligon. *Handler:* Mary Dukes. By Ch. Tekoneva's Dario ex Ch. Silver Bluff Lynncrest Mezzaluna. Born 12/24/95. Bitch. *Judge:* Mrs. Eleanor L. Rotman.
AKC Record: 19 Bests of Breed; 1 Group One placement.

The Italian Greyhound is very similar to the Greyhound, but much smaller and more slender in all proportions and of ideal elegance and grace. Dogs and bitches, ideally 13 to 15 inches.

BEST OF OPPOSITE SEX:
  Ch. Bo Bett's Peter Platinum. *Owners:* Pam Murphy and Carol Harris.
AWARDS OF MERIT:
  Ch. Suez Indian Paint Brush. *Owners:* Sue E. Nelson and Robin E. Nelson.
  Ch. Silver Bluff Just One Look. *Owner:* Linda Schaffer.

MALTESE
Ch. Ta-Jon's Tickle Me Silly

Breeders: Tammy and John W. Simon, Jr. *Owners:* Samuel B. and Marion W. Lawrence. *Handler:* Tammy Simon. By Ch. Pashes Beau Didley ex Ch. ta-Jon's Tickle Me Pink. Born 05/09/94. *Bitch. Judge:* Dr. Jacklyn E. Hungerland.
AKC Record: 125 Bests of Breed; 67 Group One placements; 16 Bests in Show.

The Maltese is a Toy dog covered from head to foot with a mantle of long, silky, white hair. He is gentle-mannered and affectionate, eager and sprightly in action, and, despite his size, possessed of the vigor needed for the satisfactory companion. For all his diminutive size, the Maltese seems to be without fear. His trust and affectionate responsiveness are very appealing. He is among the gentlest mannered of all little dogs, yet he is lively and playful as well as vigorous. Dogs and bitches, under 7 pounds, ideally 4 to 6 pounds.

BEST OF OPPOSITE SEX:
Ch. Rhapsody's Indecent Mystery. *Owners:* Larry and Angela Stanberry.
AWARDS OF MERIT:
Ch. Fantasia's Promises To Keep. *Owner:* Jerry Lea McConnell.
Ch. Petite Supermodel. *Owners:* Jose Cabrera, Fabian Arienti and Mary Ann Paul.

MANCHESTER TERRIER (TOY)

Ch. Alabiss Jack's Jill

Breeders: P. and P. Lapinski. *Owners:* Pat Dresser and Greg Myers. By Ch. St. Lazar's Action Jackson ex Alabiss Acapella. Born 10/06/92. Bitch. *Judge:* Mrs. Eleanor L. Rotman.
AKC Record: 319 Bests of Breed, including Westminster Kennel Club 1994 and 1996; 39 Group One placements; 5 Bests in Show.

A small, black, short-coated dog with distinctive rich mahogany markings and a taper style tail. In structure the Manchester presents a sleek, sturdy, yet elegant look, and has a wedge, long and clean head with a keen, bright, alert expression. The Manchester Terrier is neither aggressive nor shy. He is keenly observant, devoted but discerning. Not being a sparring breed, the Manchester is generally friendly with other dogs. Dogs and bitches, not to exceed 12 pounds.

BEST OF OPPOSITE SEX:
    Ch. Bryans Zeus The Duce. *Owners:* Joanna Satalino and Barbara Bryan.
AWARD OF MERIT:
    Ch. Salutaire Show No Mercy. *Owners:* Mrytle Klensch and Peter Rank.

MINIATURE PINSCHER

Ch. Carovels Jacobs Ladder

Breeder: Caroline Ofenloch. *Owners:* Jeffrey P. Helming and Philip A. Helming. *Handler:* Joy S. Brewster, CPH/PHA. By Ch. Sanbrook Flashy Silks ex Ch. Carovels Queen Annes Lace. Born 09/05/93. Dog. Judge: Mr. R. Stephen Shaw.
AKC Record: 181 Bests in Breed; 12 Group One placements; 1 Best in Show.

The Miniature Pinscher is structurally a well balanced, sturdy, compact, short-coupled, smooth-coated dog. He naturally is well groomed, proud, vigorous and alert. Characteristic traits are his hackney-like action, fearless animation, complete self-possession, and his spirited presence. Dogs and bitches, 10 to 12½ inches.

BEST OF OPPOSITE SEX:
    Ch. Marlex Mercedes. *Owner:* Armando Angelbello.
AWARDS OF MERIT:
    Ch. Dynasty's Jackie's Surprise. *Owners:* Helen Chrysler Greene and Jack F. Chrysler Jr.
    Ch. Whitehouse's Oh Danny Boy. *Owner:* Sandee White.
    Ch. Rising Star Tuckered Out. *Owner:* William S. Bratt.

PAPILLON

Ch. Loteki Good Time Charlie

Breeder: Lou Ann King. *Owners:* Pamela Norberg and Lou Ann King. *Handler:* Janet Bottorff. By Ch. Loteki Party Animal ex Ch. Loteki By Good Fortune. Born 04/11/94. Dog. *Judge:* Dr. Jacklyn E. Hungerland. *AKC Record:* 38 Bests of Breed; 4 Group One placements.

The Papillon is a small, friendly, elegant Toy dog of fine-boned structure, light, dainty and of lively action; distinguished from other breeds by its beautiful butterfly-like ears. In temperament, happy, alert and friendly. Neither shy nor aggressive. Dogs and bitches, 8 to 11 inches.

BEST OF OPPOSITE SEX:
Ch. Tuinluv-N-Marquis Protege' Su. *Owners:* Tina and David Moran and Dr. Keith and Nikole Whitehead.
AWARDS OF MERIT:
Ch. Loteki Supernatural Being. *Owners:* John Oulton and Lou Ann King.
Ch. Envy My Fuzzy Atta'Che. *Owners:* Ruth Ann Ramsey and Diana and Edward Fuchs.

PEKINGESE

Ch. Windemere Peterpiper Singlee

Breeders: Joy Thomas and Robert and Janet Jacobson. *Owners:* Herbert and Erna Holcombe. *Handler:* Brenda Scheiblauer. By Ch. Yakee A Town Called Malice ex Ch. Windemere's Kiss The Sun. Born 10/17/93. Dog. *Judge:* Dr. Jacklyn E. Hungerland.
AKC Record: 108 Bests of Breed; 41 Group One placements; 6 Bests in Show.

The expression must suggest the Chinese origin of the Pekingese in its quaintness and individuality, resemblance to the lion in directions and independence and should imply courage, boldness, self-esteem and combativeness rather than prettiness, daintiness or delicacy. Dogs and bitches, not to exceed 14 pounds.

BEST OF OPPOSITE SEX:
Ch. Pequest Social Butterfly. *Owner:* Julia P. Gasow.
AWARDS OF MERIT:
Ch. Kings Court Social Lion. *Owner:* James King.
Ch. Pequest Picasso. *Owners:* Mr. and Mrs. Paul G. Burghardt.

POMERANIAN
Ch. Rubys Lovely Standin Ovation

Breeders: Ruby F. Poole and Victoria E. Lovely. *Owner:* Ruby F. Poole. *Handler:* Blake Jones. By Ch. Ruby's One Man Show Encore ex Ruby's Charming Maiden Of OK. Born 12/03/94. Dog. *Judge:* Mr. Richard L. Bauer.
AKC Record: 15 Bests of Breed.

The Pomeranian in build and appearance is a cobby, balanced, short-coupled dog. He exhibits great intelligence in his expression, and is alert in character and deportment. Dogs and bitches, 3 to 7 pounds, ideally 4 to 5 pounds.

BEST OF OPPOSITE SEX:
  Ch. Valcopy-Wakhan Hot Gossip. *Owners:* Satoshi Bessho, Hideko W. Strasbaugh and Dana L. Plonkey.
AWARDS OF MERIT:
  Ch. Starfire's Superman. *Owners:* Jose Cabrera and Faviani Areinti.
  Ch. Jessica's Jessie James. *Owner:* Jessica Smith.
  Ch. Creiders Prince Dom Perignon. *Owners:* Marvin R. and Margo Koga.
  Ch. Lovely Debutante Finale. *Owner:* Victoria E. Lovely.

POODLE
(TOY)

Ch. Dignity Of Jewelry House Yoko

Breeder: Yoko Kamiya. *Owner:* Kaz Hosaka. *Handler:* Kaz Hosaka. By Ch. Wissfire Knock On Wood ex Yankee Girl Of Beau Fair Lady. Born 05/05/94. Dog. *Judge:* Mr. Richard L. Bauer.
AKC Record: 8 Bests of Breed; 2 Group One placements.

A very active, intelligent and elegant appearing dog, squarely built, well proportioned, moving soundly and carrying himself proudly. Properly clipped in the traditional fashion and carefully groomed, the Poodle has about him an air of distinction and dignity peculiar to himself. Dogs and bitches, 10 inches and under.

BEST OF OPPOSITE SEX:
Ch. Southampton One Touch O'Class. *Owners:* Stephanie Steinbrecher and Brenda Elmer.
AWARDS OF MERIT:
Ch. Advantage Ahs. *Owners:* Ray and Valerie Stevens and Gary Wittmeier.
Ch. Laurelbury Very Very Saks. *Owners:* Carole Ann Robrish and Tawnya Bobst.

GROUP 3

PUG

Ch. Neu's Chauncelear JB Rare

Breeder: Patricia Park. *Owner:* Sonja Neu. *Handler:* Corky Vroom. By Ch. Neu's Invincible Fire Lord ex Ch. Chancelor Mornin' Glory. Born 03/22/94. Dog. *Judge:* Mr. R. William Taylor.
AKC Record: 93 Bests of Breed, including Westminster Kennel Club 1996; 30 Group One placements; 4 Bests in Show.

Symmetry and general appearance are decidely square and cobby. This is an even-tempered breed, exhibiting stability, playfulness, great charm, dignity, and an outgoing, loving disposition. Dogs and bitches, 14 to 18 pounds.

BEST OF OPPOSITE SEX:
Ch. Sycamore's Juzz Divine. *Owners:* Riney C. and Alicia Kahler.
AWARDS OF MERIT:
Ch. Abelarm Cutting Edge. *Owner:* Mrs. Alan Robson.
Ch. Neu's Renaissance Man Of Mine. *Owner:* Jessie Fassanella.
Ch. Cotswold Monique. *Owner:* Janet E. Ulakovic.
Ch. Gas Hollow's Huzzah. *Owners:* Olive and Candie Brown.

SHIH TZU

Ch. Beswicks In The Nick Of Time

Breeder: Pat Waters. *Owners:* Linda and Roy Ward. *Handler:* Luke Ehricht. By Ch. Beswicks Time Out ex My Toy Dark Dancer At Beswick. Born 02/25/95. Dog. *Judge:* Mr. R. William Taylor.
AKC Record: 90 Bests of Breed; 43 Group One placements; 7 Bests in Show.

GROUP 2

The Shih Tzu is a sturdy, lively, alert Toy dog with long flowing double coat. Befitting his noble Chinese ancestry as a highly valued, prized companion and palace pet, the Shih Tzu is proud of bearing, has a distinctively arrogant carriage with head well up and tail curved over the back. As the sole purpose of the Shih Tzu is that of a companion and house pet, it is essential that its temperament be outgoing, happy, affectionate, friendly and trusting towards all. Dogs and bitches, ideally 9 to 10½ inches, ideally 9 to 16 pounds.

BEST OF OPPOSITE SEX:
  Ch. Wang's Taco Belle. *Owner:* Douglas Wang.
AWARDS OF MERIT:
  Ch. Ista's Wicked Reputation. *Owners:* Heidi and Dean Selvig.
  Ch. Grenoville Rainbows End. *Owners:* Clare Blasinski and Melissa Papke.

SILKY TERRIER
Ch. Derringdew Lucknow Winston

Breeders: Ann V. and Robert C. Leitz III. *Owners:* John P. Scheidt and Donald M. Spear. *Handler:* Barbara Heckerman. By Ch. Lucknow Local Talent ex Ch. Lucknow Totally Tuppence. Born 11/06/91. Dog. *Judge:* Mr. R. William Taylor.
AKC Record: 187 Bests of Breed, including Westminster Kennel Club 1995; 17 Group One placements.

The Silky Terrier is a true "toy terrier." He is moderately low set, slightly longer than tall, of refined bone structure, but of sufficient substance to suggest the ability to hunt and kill domestic rodents. His inquisitive nature and joy of life make him an ideal companion. The keenly alert air of the terrier is characteristic. The manner is quick, friendly, responsive. Dogs and bitches, 9 to 10 inches.

BEST OF OPPOSITE SEX:
Ch. Silkyence Jazzy Jade. *Owner:* Janice Chaffin-Bell.
AWARD OF MERIT:
Ch. Shalee Tawny Mist Royal Silk. *Owner:* Shauna L. Jones.

YORKSHIRE TERRIER
Ch. I'm The First De Penghibur

Breeder: Marguerite Gerard. *Owners:* Norman Odium and Barbara Beissel. *Handler:* Carole Cousin. By Ch. Hooligan De Penghibur ex Exctasy De Penghibur. Born 11/24/93. Bitch. *Judge:* Mr. R. Stephen Shaw.

In general appearance, that of a long-haired toy terrier whose blue and tan coat is parted on the face and from the base of the skull to the end of the tail and hangs evenly and quite straight down each side of the body. The body is neat, compact and well proportioned. The dog's high head carriage and confident manner should give the appearance of vigor and self-importance. He is very spirited and rather independent—not a lap dog, per se, but a true toy terrier. Dogs and bitches, not to exceed 7 pounds.

BEST OF OPPOSITE SEX:
   Ch. Pennylane's On The Target. *Owner:* Barbara Irwin.
AWARDS OF MERIT:
   Ch. This Time Portfolio. *Owner:* Bill Hinds.
   Ch. Cheyenne's Okie Dokie. *Owner:* Dorothy Sims.
   Ch. Bluebell's Luis Vuitton. *Owners:* Jerry and Phyllis Ross.

NON-SPORTING DOGS

At the earliest dog shows only dogs used for sporting purposes were exhibited. Later, the rarer breeds were shown in what was called a "non-sporting" category.

As time went by this group was divided into other categories: the toy dogs, the working dogs, the terriers, and the hounds. The Non-Sporting designation remained for those dogs who outlived their original purpose, such as the Bulldog, developed for bull-baiting, or the Dalmatian, a coach dog. These and other non-sporting dogs are interesting as examples of a heritage from the past. Though developed for other times, these dogs continue to be among the most popular of breeds.

There are 17 breeds or varieties in the Non-Sporting Group:

American Eskimo Dog
Bichon Frise
Boston Terrier
Bulldog
Chinese Shar-Pei
Chow Chow
Dalmatian
Finnish Spitz
French Bulldog
Keeshond
Lhasa Apso
Poodle (Miniature)
Poodle (Standard)
Schipperke
Shiba Inu
Tibetan Spaniel
Tibetan Terrier

BICHON FRISE

Ch. Sterling Rumor Has It

Breeders: Paul A. Flores, Sherrie Swarts and Nadine Minsky. *Owners:* Meriko Tamaki and Paul A. Flores. *Handler:* Paul A. Flores. By Ch. Dibett Pal Joey ex Ch. Mon Ami Chloe D. Born 11/12/93. Dog. *Judge:* Dr. Jacklyn E. Hungerland.
AKC Record: 132 Bests of Breed, including Westminster Kennel Club 1996; 40 Group One placements; 5 Bests in Show.

The Bichon Frise is a small, sturdy, white powder puff of a dog whose merry temperament is evidenced by his plumed tail carried jauntily over the back and his dark-eyed inquisitive expression. Gentle mannered, sensitive, playful and affectionate in temperament. A cheerful attitude is the hallmark of the breed and one should settle for nothing less. Dogs and bitches, 9½ to 11½ inches.

GROUP 4

BEST OF OPPOSITE SEX:
Ch. Vogelflight Banana Pudding. *Owners:* Mary M. and Kathie D. Vogel.
AWARDS OF MERIT:
Ch. Paw Mark's Fire And Ice. *Owners:* Cecelia Ruggles and Pauline Schultz.
Ch. Vilors Vassaly's Dust Buster. *Owner:* Eleanor McDonald.
Ch. Dreams Came True's Triumph. *Owner:* Mimi Winkler.

BOSTON TERRIER

Ch. Winston's Go Get'm Joey Kocur

Breeders: Dr. Alan E. and Linda Spinner. *Owners:* Dr. Alan E. and Linda Spinner and Thomas E. Daniels. *Handler:* By Ch. Crockett's Kahlua And Coffee, CDX ex Ch. Startimes Galaxy Starbaby. Born 09/03/94. Dog. *Judge:* Mr. Phillip A. Lanard III.
AKC Record: 83 Bests of Breed; 1 Group One placement.

The Boston Terrier is a lively, highly intelligent, smooth coated, short-headed, compactly built, short-tailed, well balanced dog. The dog conveys an impression of determination, strength and activity, with style of a high order; carriage easy and graceful. The Boston Terrier is a friendly and lively dog. The breed has an excellent disposition and a high degree of intelligence, which makes the Boston Terrier an incomparable companion—a most dapper and charming American original. Dogs and bitches, under 15 pounds to not exceeding 25 pounds.

BEST OF OPPOSITE SEX:
  Ch. Vierra's Royal Design By Elbo. *Owners:* James and Wendy Bettis and Jeanne M. Vierra.
AWARDS OF MERIT:
  Ch. WC's Victoria's Secret Of Oui. *Owners:* S. Maxine Uzoff and W. C. Billingsley.
  Ch. Yoki-En's Sir Andrew At Mory's. *Owners:* Mary K. and Alice S. Ochiai.
  Ch. Ch. Al-Mar's Just The Fax. *Owners:* Dr. Ellen L. Kennedy and Mary Ann Gallagher.

BULLDOG

Ch. Cherokee Dakota Robert

Breeders: Robert and Mary Keller. *Owner:* Cody T. Sickle. *Handler:* Cody T. Sickle. By Ch. Prestwick Gawain ex Ch. Dakota Arrogant Harriet. Born 09/18/93. Dog. *Judge:* Mr. Phillip A. Lanard III.
AKC Record: 100 Bests of Breed, including Westminster Kennel Club 1996; 31 Group One placements; 4 Bests in Show.

The perfect Bulldog must be of medium size and smooth coat; with heavy, thick-set, low-swung body, massive short faced head, wide shoulders and sturdy limbs. The general appearance and attitude should suggest great stability, vigor and strength. The disposition should be equable and kind, resolute and courageous, and demeanor should be pacific and dignified. These attributes should be countenanced by the expression and behavior. Dogs, about 50 pounds; bitches, about 40 pounds.

GROUP 2

BEST OF OPPOSITE SEX:
   Ch. Majestic's Peek-A-Boo-I-C-U. *Owner:* Cody T. Sickle.
AWARDS OF MERIT:
   Ch. CC Lexington Mr. Wonderful T W S. *Owners:* Chris and Sena Clark.
   Ch. Evergreen's Rawhide. *Owners:* Bliss Bancroft and Bliss VanGuilder.

CHINESE SHAR-PEI
Ch. Grayland's Good News Bygeorge

Breeders: Beth Gray-Harper and Kenneth Gray. *Owners:* Beth Gray-Harper and Kenneth Gray. *Handler:* Beth Gray-Harper. By Ch. Meiting Luv Won Macmurfee ex Grayland's Current Affair. Born 06/20/93. Dog. *Judge:* Mr. Phillip A. Lanard III.
AKC Record: 92 Bests of Breed; 7 Group One placements; 1 Best in Show.

An alert, dignified active, compact dog of medium size and substance, square in profile, close-coupled, the well proportioned head slightly but not overly large for the body. The short, harsh coat, the loose skin covering the head and body, the small ears, the "hippopotamus" muzzle shape and the high set tail impart to the Shar-Pei a unique look peculiar to him alone. Regal, alert, intelligent, dignified, lordly, scowling, sober and snobbish, essentially independent and somewhat standoffish with strangers, but extreme in his devotion to his family. The Shar-Pei stands firmly on the ground with a calm, confident stature. Dogs and bitches, 18 to 20 inches, 40 to 55 pounds.

BEST OF OPPOSITE SEX:
Ch. Grayland's Starlite Margaret. *Owner:* Ralph De La Fuente.
AWARDS OF MERIT:
Ch. Ming Yu A Touch Of Class. *Owner:* Linda Teitelbaum.
Ch. Shenaningans Storm Surge. *Owners:* Susan and Michael Lauer.
Ch. Grayland's Toucha Magic. *Owner:* Beth Toraason.
Ch. Chesapeake's Beam Me Up Scotty. *Owner:* Tami Luddeke.
Ch. Shintos Son Hawk Ming Yu. *Owner:* Linda Teitelbaum.

CHOW CHOW
Ch. Owlhead's Justin Your Dreams

Breeder: Frances L. Martin. *Owners:* Frances L. Martin and Michael and Linda Brantley. *Handler:* Linda Brantley. By Ch. Versaw's Star Of Justin ex Ch. Bearden's Dark And Stormee. Born 08/13/93. Dog. *Judge:* Mrs. Rose Ellen Fetter.
AKC Record: 123 Bests of Breed; 15 Group One placements; 2 Bests in Show.

An ancient breed of northern Chinese origin, this all-purpose dog was used for hunting, herding, pulling and protection of the home. While primarily a companion today, his working origin must always be remembered when assessing true Chow type. Keen intelligence, an independent spirit and innate dignity give the Chow an aura of aloofness. It is a Chow's nature to be reserved and discerning with strangers. Displays of aggression or timidity are unacceptable. Dogs and bitches, 17 to 20 inches.

AWARDS OF MERIT:
Ch. Imagine Memphis Magic Melody. *Owners:* A. and C. Bridges and K. and G. Beliew.
Ch. Mactyke's Lyon King O'United. *Owners:* Eileen Bruington and Ekarat Sangkunakup.

DALMATIAN
Ch. Spotlight's Spectacular

Breeders: Connie M. and Stephen J. Wagner. *Owner:* Mrs. Alan R. Robson. *Handler:* Dennis M. McCoy. By Ch. Tuckaway Augusta ex Ch. Spotlight's Rising Star. Born 05/02/92. Bitch. *Judge:* Mrs. Rose Ellen Fetter. *AKC Record:* 372 Bests of Breed, including Westminster Kennel Club 1995 and 1996; 282 Group One placements, including Westminster Kennel Club 1996; 66 Bests in Show.

The Dalmatian is a distinctively spotted dog; poised and alert; strong, muscular and active; free of shyness; intelligent in expression; symmetrical in outline; and without exaggeration or coarseness. The Dalmatian is capable of great endurance, combined with fair amount of speed. Temperament is stable and outgoing, yet dignified. Dogs and bitches, 19 to 23 inches.

GROUP 1

BEST OF OPPOSITE SEX:
Ch. Tuckaway Winged Foot. *Owners:* Carrie Jordan, Frances Remmele and Carole Harris.
AWARDS OF MERIT:
Ch. Dottaway's Go For The Gold. *Owners:* Susan E. Bloom and Karen E. Linsky.
Ch. Tioga Spellbound. *Owners:* Ollie F. Firuski and Sarum Kennels.

FINNISH SPITZ

Ch. Brown's 'Mikki'

Breeders: Marg G. and Tom T. Walker. *Owners:* Tom T. Walker and Kim Raleigh. *Handler:* Kim Raleigh. By Ch. Ukkoherran Taika ex Ch. Finkkila's Kura. Born 03/18/91. Dog. *Judge:* Dr. Jacklyn E. Hungerland. *AKC Record:* 160 Bests of Breed, including Westminster Kennel Club 1995 and 1996; 16 Group One placements; 1 Best in Show.

The Finnish Spitz presents a fox-like picture. The breed has long been used to hunt small game and birds. The Finnish Spitz's whole being shows liveliness, which is especially evident in the eyes, ears and tail. Active and friendly, lively and eager, faithful; brave, but cautious. Dogs, 17½ to 20 inches; bitches, 15½ to 19 inches.

> **BEST OF OPPOSITE SEX:**
> Ch. Finkkila's Ruskea. *Owners:* Sally J. Alexander and Marg G. Walker.

FRENCH BULLDOG
Ch. Bullmarket's Versace

Breeders: Carol Gavestock-Taylor and Arlie A. Toye. *Owners:* Carol Taylor and Kazumi Kurata. *Handler:* Norma Smith. By Ch. Bandog's One In A Million ex Ch. LeBull's Achey Breaky Heart. Born 11/11/95. Dog. *Judge:* Mrs. Rose Ellen Fetter.
AKC Record: 8 Bests of Breed.

The French Bulldog has the appearance of an active, intelligent, muscular dog of heavy bone, smooth coat, compactly built, and of medium or small structure. Expression alert, curious, and interested. Well behaved, adaptable, and comfortable companions with an affectionate nature and even disposition; generally active, alert and playful, but not unduly boisterous. Dogs and bitches, not to exceed 28 pounds.

BEST OF OPPOSITE SEX:
Ch. Legacy Antigua. *Owner:* Michael Loller.
AWARDS OF MERIT:
Ch. Blazin's Ironside Perry Of NRW. *Owners:* Elizabeth McNeil and Denise L. Blake.
Ch. Marianette Memor-A-Bul Edwina. *Owners:* Donald Smith and Randall Wallace.
Ch. Bushaway Lefox Eva Gabor. *Owners:* Colette Secher and Sarah W. Sweatt.

KEESHOND

Ch. Candray Camelia

Breeders: Janice A. Wanamaker and Nancy Fruit. *Owner:* Janice A. Wanamaker. *Handler:* Janice A. Wanamaker. By Ch. Kee Sam's Design For Ashbrook ex Ch. Candray Twinkle Time. Born 09/06/94. Bitch. *Judge:* Mrs. Rose Ellen Fetter.
AKC Record: 10 Bests of Breed.

The Keeshond (pronounced *kayz-hawnd*) is a natural, handsome dog of well-balanced, short-coupled body, attracting attention not only by his coloration, alert carriage, and intelligent expression but also by his stand-off coat, his richly plumed tail well curled over his back, his foxlike expression, and his small pointed ears. In temperament, the Keeshond is neither timid nor aggressive but, instead, is outgoing and friendly with both people and other dogs. The Keeshond is a lively, intelligent, alert and affectionate companion. Dogs, 18 inches; bitches, 17 inches.

BEST OF OPPOSITE SEX:
    Ch. Windrift's Summertime Blues. *Owner:* Joanne Reed.
AWARDS OF MERIT:
    Ch. Cara Absolute Proof E'Sprit. *Owners:* Heather Myers and Judy Thompson.
    Ch. Cara Ashbrook Casey Jones. *Owners:* Heather Myers and Linda Moss.

LHASA APSO

Ch. Martin's Tic-Toc Piaget Puff

Breeders: Patricia Bernardo and Daryl Martin. *Owners:* Michael A. Santora and Alan J. Loso. *Handler:* Daryl Martin. By Ch. Choctaw's Texas Bear ex Ch. Timekeeper's Tic-Toc Puff. Born 06/07/91. Dog. *Judge:* Mrs. Dorothy Welsh.
AKC Record: 143 Bests of Breed; 31 Group One placements; 1 Best in Show.

Gay and assertive, but chary of strangers, the little Lhasa Apso has never lost his characteristic of keen watchfulness, nor has he lost his hardy nature. These two features should always be developed, since they are of outstanding merit. These dogs are easily trained and responsive to kindness. To anyone they trust they are most obedient, and the beautiful dark eyes are certainly appealing as they wait for some mark of appreciation for their efforts. Dogs, about 10 to 11 inches; bitches, slightly smaller.

BEST OF OPPOSITE SEX:
Ch. Shi Rho-Hopefull's Hulabalou. *Owners:* Shirley L. Rhodes and Jeanne Hope.
AWARDS OF MERIT:
Ch. Harrow Jaro Canadian Club. *Owners:* Harlene Rowe and Judith Camacho.
Ch. Tatli's-Su's Windchaser Of Tikal. *Owner:* Elizabeth Chidley.
Ch. Lynnlaine's The Gambler. *Owners:* Jerry M. and Lynn Sabo Chapdelaine.

POODLE (MINIATURE)
Ch. Reignon Dassin Alexandra

Breeders: Joseph Vergnetti and Janet Lange. *Owners:* Joseph Vergnetti and Janet Lange. By Ch. Dassin Daniell D'Lewis ex Jay-Ens Trixie Delight. Born 09/02/95. Bitch. *Judge:* Mr. Richard L. Bauer.
AKC Record: 34 Bests of Breed; 12 Group One placements.

A very active, intelligent and elegant appearing dog, squarely built, well proportioned, moving soundly and carrying himself proudly. Properly clipped in the traditional fashion and carefully groomed, the Poodle has about him an air of distinction and dignity peculiar to himself. Dogs and bitches, over 10 inches to not exceeding 15 inches.

GROUP 3

BEST OF OPPOSITE SEX:
Ch. Kiyara Karadale Krusader. *Owner:* Ms. Shannon Duggan.
AWARD OF MERIT:
Ch. Sakura Popcorn. *Owner:* Kaz Hosaka.

POODLE (STANDARD)
Ch. Dawin High Falutin

Breeder: Linda C. Dawick. *Owner:* Linda C. Dawick. By Ch. Pamala's Manderly Spellbound ex Ch. Dawin's Blaze Of Glory. Born 03/05/91. Dog. *Judge:* Mr. Richard L. Bauer.
AKC Record: 68 Bests of Breed; 18 Group One placements; 3 Bests in Show.

A very active, intelligent and elegant appearing dog, squarely built, well proportioned, moving soundly and carrying himself proudly. Properly clipped in the traditional fashion and carefully groomed, the Poodle has about him an air of distinction and dignity peculiar to himself. Dogs and bitches, over 15 inches.

BEST OF OPPOSITE SEX:
Ch. Atalanta Nicole. *Owners:* Toni and Martin Sosnoff.
AWARDS OF MERIT:
Ch. Torpaz Take That. *Owner:* Nancy McGee.
Ch. Kaylen's Cadillac Style. *Owners:* Warren and Norvel Benoit and Kay L. Palade.

SCHIPPERKE

Ch. Dotsus Further More Trouble

Breeder: Brenda S. Bible. *Owner:* Chandler Hahn. *Handler:* Chandler Hahn. By Ch. Nanhall's Charbonne, CD ex Ch. Nanhall's Lake Country. Born 02/25/92. Dog. *Judge:* Mrs. Dorothy Welsh.
AKC Record: 213 Bests of Breed, including Westminster Kennel Club 1995 and 1996; 26 Group One placements; 5 Bests in Show.

The Schipperke is an agile, active watchdog and hunter of vermin. In appearance he is a small, thickset, cobby, black, tailless dog, with a fox-like face. The Schipperke is curious, interested in everything around him, and is an excellent and faithful little watchdog. He is reserved with strangers and ready to protect his family and property if necessary. He displays a confident and independent personality, reflecting the breed's original purpose as a watchdog and hunter of vermin. Dogs, 11 to 13 inches; bitches, 10 to 12 inches.

BEST OF OPPOSITE SEX:
Ch. De Lamer's Fire Island Fox. *Owner:* Krista J. Nuovo.
AWARDS OF MERIT:
Ch. Malagold Star Evol Boweebol. *Owners:* Blake Hart and Michael Starr.
Ch. Dideb's Speedeau Druex. *Owners:* Debra Dellamonica, Debbie Studwell and Jessica Plourde.

SHIBA INU
Ch. Frerose Otomi

Breeders: Frederick O. Duane and Diane Murphy. *Owners:* Frederick O. Duane and Diane Murphy. *Handler:* Edward J. Finnegan, Jr. By Suzuhomare Of Yoshimatsu Kensha ex Frerose's Punkin Pie. Born 07/16/93. Dog. *Judge:* Mrs. Dorothy Welsh.
AKC Record: 208 Bests of Breed, including Westminster Kennel Club 1996; 6 Group One placements.

The Shiba is a small breed dog. He is well balanced, well boned with muscles developed. His moderately compact and well furred body suggests his northern heritage. The Shiba's expression is alert and invites activity. In temperament, inquisitive, good natured, bright, active and slightly aloof at first introduction. Possesses a strong hunting instinct. Dogs, 14½ to 16½ inches; bitches, 13½ to 15½ inches.

BEST OF OPPOSITE SEX:
  Ch. Tanasea's Tsunami Of Zen. *Owners:* Mary King, Fran Wasserman and Debbie Meador.
AWARDS OF MERIT:
  Ch. Sho Go Gold Typhoon JP. *Owners:* Leslie Ann Engen and Frank Sakayeda.
  Ch. Arctura's Jenny At Taichung. *Owners:* Art and Laura Perkinson.
  Ch. Sunojo's Toshiba Go. *Owners:* Marianne Ross and Susan Norris Jones.

TIBETAN SPANIEL

Ch. Ebonstern Avalon Dandi Lion

Breeders: Becky Sumner and Cheryl Wheeler. *Owner:* Dr. Lee Nelson. *Handler:* David Harper. By Ch. Flolin's Full Flavor Of Tamzil ex Ch. Tibrokes Heart Of The Matter. Born 02/02/95. Dog. *Judge:* Mrs. Dorothy Welsh.
AKC Record: 43 Bests of Breed.

In general appearance, small, active and alert. The outline should give a well balanced appearance, slightly longer in body than the height at withers. In temperament, gay and assertive, highly intelligent, aloof with strangers. Dogs and bitches, about 10 inches, ideally 9 to 15 pounds.

BEST OF OPPOSITE SEX:
Ch. Ambrier Boda Zelicious Zima. *Owners:* Mrs. Betty Wrenn Hoggard and Mallory Cosby Driskill.
AWARD OF MERIT:
Ch. Dragonhold Gandharva. *Owners:* Cheryl A. Kelly and Diane Bernard.

TIBETAN TERRIER
Ch. Lan Lin's To The Max

Breeders: Bob LaPoca and Bette LaPoca. *Owners:* Randall Neece and Joseph Timko. *Handler:* Joseph Timko. By Ch. Char-Su Go Rockin Robin Shirgi ex Ch. Lan Lins Midnight Shadow. Born 02/05/90. Dog. *Judge:* Mr. Richard L. Bauer.
AKC Record: 50 Bests of Breed.

The Tibetan Terrier evolved over many centuries, surviving in Tibet's extreme climate and difficult terrain. The breed developed a protective double coat, compact size, unique foot construction, and great agility. The Tibetan Terrier served as a steadfast, devoted companion in all of his owner's endeavors. The Tibetan Terrier is highly intelligent, sensitive, loyal, devoted and affectionate. The breed may be cautious or reserved. Dogs and bitches, 15 to 16 inches, 18 to 30 pounds, average 20 to 24 pounds.

BEST OF OPPOSITE SEX:
    Ch. Martin's Tal Hi Ho Puff. *Owner:* Patricia Bernardo.
AWARDS OF MERIT:
    Ch. Ashlyn's Regalia Black Velvet. *Owners:* Ron and Jan Jaramillo and Jeanette Chaix.
    Ch. Regalia's Alexander The Great. *Owner:* Patricia Bernardo.
    Ch. Shalu Atisha's Magic Firebird. *Owners:* S. Rutledge, L. Schulties and M. DeMers.

HERDING DOGS

The herding instinct that made the wolf a successful hunter was recognized by man and adapted to his advantage. Domesticated and specialized through selective breeding, they evolved into the herding dogs that made successful farming possible. The great agricultural lands could never have been settled without him, and to this day he works side by side with man. These dogs are agile in movement, anticipating every move, able to turn in an instant, acting on their own or in response to a signal, "eyeing" their flock into obedience. Even those whose versatility extends to working as draft animals or guard dogs may be powerfully built, but never are they cumbersome.

There are 17 breeds or varieties in the Herding Group:

Australian Cattle Dog
Australian Shepherd
Bearded Collie
Belgian Malinois
Belgian Sheepdog
Belgian Tervuren
Border Collie
Bouvier des Flandres
Briard
Collie (Rough)
Collie (Smooth)
German Shepherd Dog
Old English Sheepdog
Puli
Shetland Sheepdog
Welsh Corgi (Cardigan)
Welsh Corgi (Pembroke)

AUSTRALIAN CATTLE DOG

Ch. Rochan's Bronc Buster, CD

Breeders: Barbara Peterson and Randall Hodge. *Owners:* Joyce Rowland, Ellen Keys, Barbara Peterson and Randall Hodge. *Handler:* Kim Griffith. By Ch. Dawn Heirs Blu Bronco ex Ch. Shurcan Lite Yer Fire. Born 02/15/91. Dog. *Judge:* Mrs. Lynette J. Saltzman.
AKC Record: 128 Bests of Breed.

The general appearance is that of a sturdy, compact, symmetrically built working dog. With the ability and willingness to carry out any task however arduous, its combination of substance, power, balance and hard muscular condition to be such that must convey the impression of great agility, strength and endurance. The utility purpose is assistance in the control of cattle, in both wide open and confined areas. Ever alert, extremely intelligent, watchful, courageous and trustworthy, with an implicit devotion to duty, making it an ideal dog. Its loyalty and protective instincts make it a self-appointed guardian to the stockman, his herd, his property. Whilst suspicious of strangers, it must be amenable to handling in the show ring. Dogs, 18 to 20 inches; bitches, 17 to 19 inches.

BEST OF OPPOSITE SEX:
   Ch. Moto Movers Mystic Maiden. *Owner:* Christina Nutt.
AWARDS OF MERIT:
   Ch. Carben Copy Truth Be Told. *Owners:* Tracy and Doug Carlton.
   Ch. Hilltop's Chilly Willy. *Owners:* Laura Lynn and Nathan Pyles.

AUSTRALIAN SHEPHERD
Ch. Briarbrooks Full Speed Ahead, PT

Breeder: L. Wilson. *Owner:* Marcia Stiger. By Ch. My Main Man Of Heatherhill ex Ch. Briarbrooks Silver Sequence. Born 07/02/92. Dog. *Judge:* Mr. Stanley S. Saltzman.
AKC Record: 117 Bests of Breed; 4 Group One placements.

The Australian Shepherd is a well-balanced dog of medium size and bone. He is attentive and animated, showing strength and stamina combined with unusual agility. The Australian Shepherd is intelligent, primarily a working dog of strong herding and guarding instincts. He is an exceptional companion. He is versatile and easily trained, performing his assigned tasks with great style and enthusiasm. He is reserved with strangers but does not exhibit shyness. Although an aggressive, authoritative worker, the Aussie must not demonstrate viciousness toward people or animals. Dogs, 20 to 23 inches; bitches, 18 to 21 inches.

BEST OF OPPOSITE SEX:
Ch. Propwash Flounce. *Owners:* Robin L. Prouty and Leslie Frank.
AWARDS OF MERIT:
Ch. Show-Me's Shadow Dancer. *Owners:* Karen and Amy Roesner.
Ch. Accolade A Toute Vitesse. *Owner:* Wendy Dreyer.
Ch. Propwash St. Elmo's Fire. *Owner:* Leslie B. Frank.
Ch. Bayshore's Flapjack. *Owners:* Frank and Linda DiSanto and J. F. Baylis.
Ch. Thornapple Hot Buttered Rum. *Owner:* Joan McIntire.

BEARDED COLLIE

Ch. Diotima Bear Necessity

Breeders: Mr. and Mrs. S.C. Appleby. *Owners:* Pat McDonald, S. Lybrand, K. and L. Swain and P. Hyde. *Handler:* Mark Bettis. By Ch. Potterdale Just William ex Ch Diotima Gabriella. Born 04/29/90. Dog. *Judge:* Mr. Michael Larizza.
AKC Record: 328 Bests of Breed, including Westminster Kennel Club 1995 and 1996; 140 Group One placements, including Westminster Kennel Club 1996; 35 Bests in Show.

The Bearded Collie is hardy and active, with an aura of strength and agility characteristic of a real working dog. Bred for centuries as a companion and servant of man, the Bearded Collie is a devoted and intelligent member of the family. He is stable and self-confident, showing no signs of shyness or aggression. This is a natural and unspoiled breed. Dogs, 21 to 22 inches; bitches, 20 to 21 inches.

BEST OF OPPOSITE SEX:
Ch. Britannia How Sweet It Is CD PT. *Owner:* Michele Ritter.
AWARDS OF MERIT:
Ch. Brigadoon's Special Edition. *Owner:* Penny Hanigan.
Ch. Brigadoon's Buffalo Soldier CD. *Owner:* Virginia Hanigan.
Ch. Chelsic Cape Breton And Me. *Owner:* Joyce Ann Burgett.

BELGIAN MALINOIS

Ch. Diadem Paragon Paladin

Breeder: Antonia Diamond. *Owner:* Antonia Diamond. *Handler:* Allan Chambers. By Ch. Diadem Paladin De Chardia ex Diadem Zenith Carbonrouge. Born 01/26/94. Dog. *Judge:* Mrs. Kathleen O. Steen. *AKC Record:* 53 Bests of Breed.

The Belgian Malinois is a well balanced, square dog, elegant in appearance with an exceedingly proud carriage of the head and neck. The breed is confident, exhibiting neither shyness nor aggressiveness in new situations. The dog may be reserved with strangers but is affectionate with his own people. He is naturally protective of his owner's person and property without being overly aggressive. The Belgian Malinois possesses a strong desire to work and is quick and responsive to commands from his owner. Dogs, 24 to 26 inches; bitches, 22 to 24 inches.

BEST OF OPPOSITE SEX:
Ch. Tri Sorts Kate. *Owners:* Hester L. Bakewell and Carol E. Knock.
AWARD OF MERIT:
Ch. Windrush's Mika Of Broadcreek. *Owners:* Susan and Chris Brendel and Dr. and Mrs. M. Kornfeld.
Ch. Tri Sorts Bold Retainer. *Owners:* Lisa M. Knock, Carl Brown and Martha R. Moses.

BELGIAN SHEEPDOG

Ch. Inchallah's Russian Roulette

Breeders: Roxanne Chumbley and Heike Wehrle. *Owner:* Roxanne Chumbley. *Handler:* Laura King. By Ch. Sundown's Little Man Tate ex Bel-Reve's Quisme O'Lifelong. Born 04/15/93. Dog. *Judge:* Mrs. Kathleen O. Steen.
AKC Record: 33 Bests of Breed; 4 Group One placements.

The Belgian Sheepdog is a well balanced, square dog, elegant in appearance with an exceedingly proud carriage of the head and neck. The Belgian Sheepdog should reflect the qualities of intelligence, courage, alertness and devotion to master. To his inherent aptitude as a guardian of flocks should be added protectiveness of the person and property of his master. He should be watchful, attentive, and always in motion when not under command. In his relationship with humans, he should be observant and vigilant with strangers, but not apprehensive. He should not show fear or shyness. He should not show viciousness by unwarranted or unprovoked attack. With those he knows well, he is most affectionate and friendly, zealous of their attention and very possessive. Dogs, 24 to 26 inches; bitches, 22 to 24 inches.

BEST OF OPPOSITE SEX:
  Ch. Nordost's Mountain Laurel. *Owners:* Donna Memming, Rita Thatcher and D. Johnson.
AWARD OF MERIT:
  Ch. Bel-Reve's Pistolero. *Owners:* Cathy H. and William G. Daugherty.

BELGIAN TERVUREN

Am-Int. Ch. Mar Bo-Jac's Kool Hand Luke, CGC

Breeder: Jackie Orrell. *Owner:* Vicki Havicon. *Handler:* Vicki Havicon. By Ch. Labelle's A Liberte ex Ch. Co-Ra-Lanes Beau-Ja-Renee. Born 02/27/90. Dog. *Judge:* Mrs. Kathleen O. Steen. *AKC Record:* 186 Bests of Breed; 10 Group One placements.

The Belgian Tervuren is a well balanced, square dog, elegant in appearance with an exceedingly proud carriage of the head and neck. The Belgian Tervuren should reflect the qualities of intelligence, courage, alertness and devotion to master. To his inherent aptitude as a guardian of flocks should be added protectiveness of the person and property of his master. He should be watchful, attentive, and always in motion when not under command. In his relationship with humans, he should be observant and vigilant with strangers, but not apprehensive. He should not show fear or shyness. He should not show viciousness by unwarranted or unprovoked attack. With those he knows well, he is most affectionate and friendly, zealous of their attention and very possessive. Dogs, 24 to 26 inches; bitches, 22 to 24 inches.

BEST OF OPPOSITE SEX:
Ch. Roma De Amfravira. *Owner:* Chris Aliapoulios.
AWARD OF MERIT:
Ch. Sharvonne New Little Bigman. *Owners:* David and Liza Michicoff.

BORDER COLLIE

Aus-Am. Ch. Nahrof First Edition

Breeders: Laura Summers and E. Badior. *Owners:* Annemarie Silverton and Laura Summers. *Handler:* Bruce Schultz, CPH/PHA. By Ch. Beechwood Boots Nail ex Gotrah Celtic Bria, CD, TDX. Born 03/23/89. *Dog. Judge:* Mr. Stanley S. Saltzman.
AKC Record: 33 Bests of Breed; 4 Group One placements.

The Border Collie is a well-balanced, medium-sized dog of athletic appearance, displaying grace and agility in equal measure with substance and stamina. His hard, muscular body has a smooth outline which conveys the impression of effortless movement and endless endurance—characteristics which have made him the world's premier sheep herding dog. He is energetic, alert and eager. Intelligence is his hallmark. The Border Collie is affectionate towards friends, he may be sensibly reserved towards strangers and therefore makes an excellent watch-dog. An intensive worker while herding, he is eager to learn and to please, and thrives on human companionship. Dogs 19 to 22 inches; bitches, 18 to 21 inches.

BEST OF OPPOSITE SEX:
  Ch. Tazmanian Bandit. *Owner:* Vona Schuring.
AWARDS OF MERIT:
  Ch. Clan-Abby The Wizard Of Oz. *Owners:* Carol Rice and Warren Rice.
  Ch. Wizaland Daily Double At Darkwind. *Owners:* Lee Levy and Robyn Powley.

BRIARD

Ch. Deja Vu House On Fire

Breeder: Terry Miller. *Owners:* B. and B. Berg and T. Miller. *Handler:* Lisa Bettis. By Ch. Deja Vu Woodbine Cryn Out Loud ex Deja Vu Four Leaf Clover. Born 08/26/92. Bitch. *Judge:* Mr. Stanley S. Saltzman. *AKC Record:* 138 Bests of Breed, including Westminster Kennel Club 1996; 14 Group One placements; 2 Bests in Show.

GROUP 4

A dog of handsome form. Vigorous and alert, powerful without coarseness, strong in bone and muscle, exhibiting the strength and agility required of the herding dog. He is a dog at heart, with spirit and initiative, wise and fearless with no trace of timidity. Intelligent, easily trained, faithful, gentle, and obedient, the Briard possesses an excellent memory and an ardent desire to please his master. He retains a high degree of his ancestral instinct to guard home and master. Although he is reserved with strangers, he is loving and loyal to those he knows. Some will display a certain independence. Dogs, 23 to 27 inches; bitches, 22 to 25½ inches.

BEST OF OPPOSITE SEX:
Ch. Deja Vu Instant Success. *Owner:* Lee Davidson.
AWARDS OF MERIT:
Ch. Deja Vu Heartbreak Hotel. *Owners:* Barbara and Rainer Hengst.
Ch. L'Heureux Au Gusta Du Loup D'Or. *Owner:* Teresa Lee.

COLLIE (ROUGH)
Ch. Westwood Th' Ultimate Warrior

Breeder: Kathy Drabik. *Owner:* Kathy Drabik. By Westwood Skyhawk ex Ch. Westwood Strike A Pose. Born 05/19/94. Dog. *Judge:* Mr. Stanley S. Saltzman.
AKC Record: 4 Bests of Breed.

The Collie is a lithe, strong, responsive, active dog, carrying no useless timber, standing naturally straight and firm. The Collie presents an impressive, proud picture of true balance, each part being in harmonious proportion to every other part and to the whole. Expression (which is desirably "sweet") is one of the most important points in considering the relative value of Collies. Dogs, 24 to 26 inches, 60 to 75 pounds; bitches, 22 to 24 inches, 50 to 65 pounds.

BEST OF OPPOSITE SEX:
   Ch. Regal Radiance. *Owner:* Lucinda Marvin.
AWARD OF MERIT:
   Ch. Glenhill Argent Quantum Leap. *Owner:* Dr. Cindi Bossart.

COLLIE (SMOOTH)

Ch. Lisara Slick Chic

Breeders: Carmen L. and Lawrence Leonard. *Owners:* Debbie Price and LouAnn Young. By Ch. Lisara's Aggreth Liaison ex Lisara's Whisper In The Night. Born 03/05/91. Bitch. *Judge:* Mr. Stanley S. Saltzman. *AKC Record:* 38 Bests of Breed; 1 Group One placement.

The Collie is a lithe, strong, responsive, active dog, carrying no useless timber, standing naturally straight and firm. The Collie presents an impressive, proud picture of true balance, each part being in harmonious proportion to every other part and to the whole. Expression (which is desirably "sweet") is one of the most important points in considering the relative value of Collies. Dogs, 24 to 26 inches, 60 to 75 pounds; bitches, 22 to 24 inches, 50 to 65 pounds.

BEST OF OPPOSITE SEX:
Ch. Tedjoi D'Artagnan. Owners: Duncan and Libby Beiler.
AWARDS OF MERIT:
Ch. Olympus Bama's Nice & Sweet. Owner: Douglas D. Haloftis.
Ch. Destiny's Tinker Toy. Owner: Sheila M. Doughman.

GERMAN SHEPHERD DOG

Ch. Autumns Shaquille

Breeders: Curtis and Janie L. Shaver. *Owners:* Curtis and Janie L. Shaver. *Handler:* Kenneth L. Rayner, Jr. By Ch. Covy-Tucker Hill's Candy Man ex Oakdale's Dansk. Born 06/16/93. Dog. *Judge:* Mr. Stanley S. Saltzman.
AKC Record: 47 Bests of Breed; 3 Group One placements.

The first impression of a good German Shepherd Dog is that of a strong, agile, well muscled animal, alert and full of life. The breed has a distinct personality marked by direct and fearless, but not hostile, expression, self-confidence and a certain aloofness that does not lend itself to immediate and indiscriminate friendships. The dog must be approachable, quietly standing its ground and showing confidence and willingness to meet overtures without itself making them. It is poised, but when the occasion demands, eager and alert; both fit and willing to serve in its capacity as companion, watchdog, blind leader, herding dog, or guardian, which the circumstances demand. Dogs, 24 to 26 inches; bitches, 22 to 24 inches.

BEST OF OPPOSITE SEX:
Ch. Autumn Kings Someday Mariah. *Owners:* Deb and Henry Rodrique.
AWARD OF MERIT:
Ch. Brier Hills Splitting Image. *Owners:* Linda Jones and M. Sherr.

OLD ENGLISH SHEEPDOG

Ch. Moptop's Vested Interest

Breeders: Woody Nelson and Toni Lett. *Owners:* Woody Nelson and Ted Forehand. By Ch. Auriga's Neat Pete From ToJo ex Ch. Raffles Chelsea Buns. Born 05/10/95. Dog. *Judge:* Mr. Michael Larizza. *AKC Record:* 5 Bests of Breed; 1 Group One placement.

A strong, compact, square, balanced dog. Taking him all around, he is pro- fusely, *but not excessively coated,* thickset, muscular and able bodied. These qualities, combined with his agil- ity, fit him for the demanding tasks required of a shepherd's or drover's dog. An adaptable, intelligent dog of even disposition, with no sign of aggression, shyness or nervousness. Dogs, 22 inches; bitches, 21 inches.

BEST OF OPPOSITE SEX:
Ch. Whisperwood's Whoopdedo. *Owners:* Joyce Wetzler and Linda Ruelle.
AWARDS OF MERIT:
Ch. Bahlamb's Blazing Banner. *Owners:* Amy Howard and Suzanne Ersson.
Ch. Lambluv's Desert Dancer. *Owners:* Keiko Lasceitles and Jere Marder.

PULI

Ch. Prydain Masterpiece, PT

Breeders: Barbara Edwards and L. Leland. *Owners:* Susan McConnell and B. Edwards. *Handler:* Susan McConnell. By Ch. Trumpkin Al Dente ex Ch. Prydain Zabi. Born 11/29/90. Dog. *Judge:* Mrs. Cate Eliz Cartledge.
AKC Record: 84 Bests of Breed; 10 Group One placements; 2 Bests in Show.

The Puli is a compact, square appearing, well balanced dog of medium size. He is vigorous, alert and active. Striking and highly characteristic is the shaggy coat which, combined with his light-footed, distinctive movement, has fitted him for the strenuous work of herding flocks on the plains of Hungary. Agility, combined with soundness of mind and body, is of prime importance for the proper fulfillment of this centuries-old task. By nature an affectionate, intelligent and home-loving companion, the Puli is sensibly suspicious and therefore an excellent watchdog. Dogs, ideally 17 inches; bitches, 16 inches.

BEST OF OPPOSITE SEX:
  Ch. Prydain Empress Erzsebet. *Owners:* C. Davidson, E. Ostermeier and B. Edwards.
AWARD OF MERIT:
  Ch. Prydain Knockout. *Owners:* Steve and Alice Lawrence and Barbara Edwards.

SHETLAND SHEEPDOG
Ch. Zion's Man About Town

Breeders: Shirley Vicchitto and Stephen V. Vicchitto. *Owner:* Madelaine Griffin-Cone. *Handler:* Linda Guihen. By Ch. Kylene Cinda Hope Town Cryer ex Zion's Tuff-E-Nuff. Born 04/09/94. Dog. *Judge:* Mr. Stanley S. Saltzman.
AKC Record: 97 Bests of Breed; 18 Group One placements; 3 Bests in Show.

The Shetland Sheepdog, like the Collie, traces to the Border Collie of Scotland, which, transported to the Shetland Islands and crossed with small, intelligent, longhaired breeds, was reduced to miniature proportions. Subsequently crosses were made from time to time with Collies. This breed now bears the same relationship in size and general appearance to the Rough Collie as the Shetland Pony does to some of the larger breeds of horses. The Shetland Sheepdog is intensely loyal, affectionate, and responsive to his owner. However, he may be reserved toward strangers but not to the point of showing fear or cringing in the ring. Dogs and bitches, 13 to 16 inches.

GROUP 1

BEST OF OPPOSITE SEX:
    Ch. Fran-Dor's Kelcie. *Owners:* Carol Arteta and Doris Homsher.
AWARDS OF MERIT:
    Ch. Hannalore Tiger Rag. *Owner:* Aneita L. Frey.
    Ch. Gemstone Sea Of Love. *Owners:* Melvin P. Cohen and Evon C. Cohen.

WELSH CORGI (CARDIGAN)

Ch. Rhydowen Jasper Tewdwyr, HS

Breeders: Rhydowen Kennels, D. Lawrence and W. Bugdorf. *Owners:* Eileen T. Dugan and Rhydowen Kennels. *Handlers:* Pat Santi and Alan Levine. By Ch. Rhydowen Philadelphia Flash ex Rhydowen Riverview Cassie. Born 01/13/92. Dog. *Judge:* Mrs. Cate Eliz Cartledge.
AKC Record: 138 Bests of Breed; 1 Group One placement.

A handsome, powerful, small dog, capable of both speed and endurance, intelligent, sturdily built but not coarse. In temperament, even-tempered, loyal, affectionate and adaptable. Never shy nor vicious. Dogs, 10½ to 12½ inches, 30 to 38 pounds; bitches, 10½ to 12½ inches, 25 to 34 pounds.

BEST OF OPPOSITE SEX:
    Ch. Kingsbury's Carbon Copy. *Owner:* Jacque Schatz.
AWARDS OF MERIT:
    Ch. McLea's Admiral. *Owner:* Leah James.
    Ch. Springshire's Brieannan. *Owner:* Stuart H. Lease.
    Ch. Garrett's Special Legend Of Grangefld. *Owner:* Shirley Hobbs.

WELSH CORGI (PEM-BROKE)

Ch. Just Enuff Of The Real Thing

Breeders: Susan L. Klar and Kathleen A. Broska. *Owners:* Olga Goizueta Rawls and Roberto C. Goizueta. *Handler:* Rebecca T. Lycan. By Ch. Nebriowa The Real Thing ex Ch. Arbor Just Enuff Double Talk, CD. Born 08/08/93. Dog. *Judge:* Mrs. Cate Eliz Cartledge. *AKC Record:* 152 Bests of Breed, including Westminster Kennel Club 1996; 50 Group One placements; 9 Bests in Show.

GROUP 3

Low-set, strong, sturdily built and active, giving an impression of substance and stamina in a small space. Outlook bold, but kindly. Expression intelligent and interested. Dogs, 10 to 12 inches, approximately 27 pounds; bitches, 10 to 12 inches, approximately 25 pounds.

BEST OF OPPOSITE SEX:
Ch. Nebriowa Saddle Lane Arribba. *Owners:* Mrs. Alan R. Robson, Ruth Cooper and Tim Mathiesen.

AWARDS OF MERIT:
Ch. Jade Tree Penway Up Country HC. *Owners:* Mary Day, Chris Johnson and Sylvia Lueck, DVM.
Ch. Heronsway Heartbeat. *Owner:* Mrs. Anne H. Bowes.
Ch. Valleyvixens Sunrunner Colors. *Owner:* Martha B. Ihrman.

NOT PICTURED
SPORTING DOGS

Spaniel (Cocker) Black
Ch. OSage's Fly Boy

Breeder: Doris Conrad. *Owner*: Doris Conrad. By Ch. Tamra's Top Gun ex Ch. Osage's Sundance Stole-N-Mink. Born 08/19/92. Dog. *Judge*: Mr. James E. Frank.

BEST OF OPPOSITE SEX:
Ch. Glen Abbey's Wild Card. *Owners*: Mary Maloney and Lee Bergstrom.
AWARDS OF MERIT:
Ch. Cary's Soul Mate. *Owners*: Jim and Kathy Van Elswyk and Carol Papp.
Ch. Milro's Barrister Alibi. *Owners*: Thomas E. Campbell and Bettie A. Campbell.

TERRIER DOGS

Irish Terrier
Ch. Rockledge's Mick Of Meath

Breeder: Linda Honey. *Owners*: Linda and Marion Honey. By Ch. Mullaghboy Colin Murphy ex Ch. Glen Kelly Maeve O'Rockledge. Born 07/20/93. Dog. *Judge*: Mrs. Sandra Goose Allen.

BEST OF OPPOSITE SEX:
Ch. Long Hill Hearts On Fire. *Owners*: Don Brouilette and Stan Wojewodski Jr.
AWARD OF MERIT:
Ch. Bally Riche Cave Canem. *Owners*: Robert F. Wynne and Joyce Wilson.

Soft Coated Wheaten Terrier
Ch. Paisley Midnight Sun

Breeders: Kathleen Margaret and Mary Evelyn McIndoe. *Owners*: Kathleen Margaret and Mary Evelyn McIndoe. By Ch. Paisley After Midnight ex Ch. Paisley Temptation Eyes. Born 04/24/93. Dog. *Judge*: Mrs. Anne S. Katona.

BEST OF OPPOSITE SEX:
Ch. Oakhollow-Kerryglen Model T. *Owners*: Marcia Stanger and Bob Stanger.
AWARDS OF MERIT:
Ch. Greentree Brin Starmaker. *Owners*: B. and S. Sarnowski, B. Trapani and K. McDonald.
Ch. Andover Make A Wish. *Owner*: Jacqueline Gottlieb.

Welsh Terrier
Ch. Anasazi Billy The Kid

Breeders: Michael and Nancy O'Neal. *Owners*: R. Schwartz. By Ch. Anasazi Trail Boss ex Ch. La Sierra's Latest Choice. Born 05/13/92. Dog. *Judge*: Dr. Robert J. Berndt.

BEST OF OPPOSITE SEX:
Ch. Celtic Lady Fergussyn. *Owners*: Cathy Gaskell and Gary and Patricia Stowell.
AWARD OF MERIT:
Ch. Kirkwood Top Brass. *Owner*: Frank Stevens.

TOY DOGS

Japanese Chin
Ch. Briarhill Rock And Roll

Breeder: Geraldine B. Craddock. *Owners*: Diane L. Meyer and Geraldine B. Craddock. By Ch. Ytaeb's Aka-Chan ex Ch. Briarhill Honeysuckle Rose. Born 11/11/93. Dog. *Judge*: Mr. R. William Taylor.

BEST OF OPPOSITE SEX:
Ch. Hillviews Tenyko V Elmac. *Owner*: Christine Salyers.
AWARDS OF MERIT:
Ch. Kikichans Bagheera. *Owners*: Bob and Margaret Sheehan.
Ch. Chindales Just A Rumor. *Owners*: Dale and Vincent Adams.

NON SPORTING DOGS

American Eskimo
Ch. Sierra's Orion

Breeder: Diana L. Allen. *Owner*: C. Anne Bishop, PHD. By Sierra's Sudden Fame ex Sierra's Showstopper. Born 12/21/92. Dog. *Judge*: Mr. Phillip A. Lanard III.

BEST OF OPPOSITE SEX:
Ch. Jaybar Cir-B Phoebe's Katidid. *Owners*: J.T. Brothers and B. Blackwood.
AWARD OF MERIT:
Ch. Fox' Loaded Dice Of Starr. *Owner*: Debbie Fox.

HERDING DOGS

Bouvier des Flandres
Ch. Terra's Too Hot To Handle

Breeder: Terry Burian. *Owners*: Lee Lochhead and Terry Burian. By Ch. Galbraith's Ironeyes ex Ch. Terra's Starry Starry Night. Born 08/19/94. Bitch. *Judge*: Mrs. Kathleen O. Steen.

BEST OF OPPOSITE SEX:
Ch. Rocheuses Extra On Stage. *Owners*: Dave Foose and Doug and Micheal Anne Johnson.
AWARDS OF MERIT:
Ch. Amber Mist Tino Falsca War. *Owners*: Debbie and Steve Potter.
Ch. Galbraith's Eye Spy. *Owners*: Bo Blanton and Jay Van Dwingelen.
Ch. Quiche's Some Like It Hot. *Owners*: Jeffrey Bennett and Nan Bennett.

The National Junior Showmanship Finals take place at Westminster each year. This competition attracts the best young handlers from around the country. This year 127 Juniors were entered.

WKC BEST IN SHOW AWARDS

1907	Winthrop Rutherfurd—Ch. Warren Remedy, Smooth Fox Terrier
1908	Winthrop Rutherfurd—Ch. Warren Remedy, Smooth Fox Terrier
1909	Winthrop Rutherfurd—Ch. Warren Remedy, Smooth Fox Terrier
1910	Sabine Kennels—Ch. Sabine Rarebit, Smooth Fox Terrier
1911	A. Albright, Jr.—Ch. Tickle Em Jock, Scottish Terrier
1912	William P. Wolcott—Ch. Kenmare Sorceress, Airedale Terrier
1913	Alex H. Stewart—Ch. Strathtay Prince Albert, Bulldog
1914	Mrs. Tylor Morse—Ch. Slumber, Old English Sheepdog
1915	George W. Quintard—Ch. Matford Vic, Wire Fox Terrier
1916	George W. Quintard—Ch. Matford Vic, Wire Fox Terrier
1917	Mrs. Roy A. Rainey—Ch. Conejo Wycollar Boy, Wire Fox Terrier
1918	R.H. Elliot—Ch. Haymarket Faultless, Bull Terrier
1919	G.L. Davis—Ch. Briergate Bright Beauty, Airedale Terrier
1920	Mrs. Roy A. Rainey—Ch. Conejo Wycollar Boy, Wire Fox Terrier
1921	William T. Payne—Ch. Midkiff Seductive, Cocker Spaniel
1922	Frederic C. Hodd—Ch. Boxwood Barkentine, Airedale Terrier
1923	There was no BEST IN SHOW award this year.
1924	Bayard Warren—Ch. Barberryhill Bootlegger, Sealyham Terrier
1925	Robert F. Maloney—Ch. Governor Moscow, Pointer
1926	Halleston Kennels—Ch. Signal Circuit of Halleston, Wire Fox Terrier
1927	Frederic C. Brown—Ch. Pinegrade Perfection, Sealyham Terrier
1928	R.M. Lewis—Ch. Talavera Margaret, Wire Fox Terrier
1929	Mrs. Florence B. Ilch-Laund Loyalty of Bellhaven, Collie
1930	John G. Bates—Ch. Pendley Calling of Blarney, Wire Fox Terrier
1931	John G. Bates—Ch. Pendley Calling of Blarney, Wire Fox Terrier
1932	Giralda Farms—Ch. Nancolleth Markable, Pointer
1933	S.M. Stewart—Ch. Warland Protector of Shelterock, Airedale Terrier
1934	Halleston Kennels—Ch. Flornell Spicy Bit of Halleston, Wire Fox Terrier
1935	Blakeen Kennels—Ch. Nunsoe Duc de la Terrace of Blakeen, Standard Poodle
1936	Claredale Kennels—Ch. St. Margaret Mignificent of Claredale, Sealyham Terrier
1937	Halleston Kennels—Ch. Flornell Spicey, Piece of Halleston, Wire Fox Terrier
1938	Maridor Kennels—Ch. Daro of Maridor, English Setter
1939	Giralda Farms—Ch. Ferry v. Rauhfelsen of Giralda, Doberman Pinscher
1940	H.E. Mellenthin—Ch. My Own Brucie, Cocker Spaniel
1941	H.E. Mellenthin—Ch. My Own Brucie, Cocker Spaniel
1942	Mrs. J.G. Winant—Ch. Wolvey Pattern of Edgerstoune, West Highland White Terrier
1943	Mrs. P.H.B. Frelinghuysen—Ch. Pitter Patter of Piperscroft, Miniature Poodle
1944	Mrs. Edward P. Alker-Flornell-Rare-Bit of Twin Ponds, Welsh Terrier
1945	Mr. & Mrs. T.H. Snethen—Ch. Shieling's Signature, Scottish Terrier
1946	Mr. & Mrs. T.H. Carruthers III—Ch. Heatherington Model Rhythm, Wire Fox Terrier
1947	Mr. & Mrs. Richard C. Kettles, Jr.—Ch. Warlord of Mazelaine, Boxer
1948	Mr. & Mrs. William A. Rockefeller—Ch. Rock Ridge Night Rocket, Bedlington Terrier
1949	Mr. & Mrs. John Phelps Wagner—Ch. Mazelaine Zazarac Brandy, Boxer
1950	Mrs. J.G. Winant—Ch. Walsing Winning Trick of Edgerstoune, Scottish Terrier
1951	Dr. & Mrs. R.C. Harris—Ch. Bang Away of Sirrah Crest, Boxer

1952	Mr. & Mrs. Len Carey—Ch. Rancho Dobe's Storm, Doberman Pinscher
1953	Mr. & Mrs. Len Carey—Ch. Rancho Dobe's Storm, Doberman Pinscher
1954	Mrs. Carl E. Morgan—Ch. Carmor's Rise and Shine, Cocker Spaniel
1955	John A. Saylor, MD—Ch. Kippax Feamought, Bulldog
1956	Bertha Smith—Ch. Wilber White Swan, Toy Poodle
1957	Sunny Shay and Dorothy Chenade—Ch. Shirkhan of Grandeur, Afghan Hound
1958	Puttencove Kennels—Ch. Puttencove Promise, Standard Poodle
1959	Dunwalke Kennels—Ch. Fontclair Festoon, Miniature Poodle
1960	Mr. & Mrs. C.C. Venable—Ch. Chik T'Sun of Caversham, Pekingese
1961	Miss Florence Michelson—Ch. Cappoquin Little Sister, Toy Poodle
1962	Wishing Well Kennels—Ch. Elfinbrook Simon, West Highland White Terrier
1963	Mrs. W.J.S. Borie—Ch. Wakefield's Black Knight, English Springer Spaniel
1964	Pennyworth Kennels—Ch. Courtenay Fleetfoot of Pennyworth, Whippet
1965	Mr. & Mrs. Charles C. Stalter—Ch. Carmichaels Fanfare, Scottish Terrier
1966	Marion G. Bunker—Ch. Zeloy, Mooremaide's Magic, Wire Fox Terrier
1967	E.H. Stuart—Ch. Bardene Bingo, Scottish Terrier
1968	Mr. & Mrs. James A. Farrell, Jr.—Ch. Stingray of Derryabah, Lakeland Terrier
1969	Walter F. Goodman & Mrs. Adele Goodman—Ch. Glamoor Good News, Skye Terrier
1970	Dr. & Mrs. P.J. Pagano & Dr. Theodore Fickes—Ch. Arriba's Prima Donna, Boxer
1971	Milton E. Prickett—Ch. Chinoe's Adamant James, English Springer Spaniel
1972	Milton E. Prickett—Ch. Chinoe's Adamant James, English Springer Spaniel
1973	Edward Jenner & Jo Ann Sering—Ch. Acadia Command Performance, Standard Poodle
1974	Richard P. Smith, MD—Ch. Gretchenhof Columbia River, German Shorthaired Pointer
1975	Mr. & Mrs. R. Vanword—Ch. Sir Lancelot of Barvan, Old English Sheepdog
1976	Mrs. V.K. Dickson—Ch. Jo Ni's Red Baron of Crofton, Lakeland Terrier
1977	Pool Forge Kennels—Ch. Dersade Bobby's Girl, Sealyham Terrier
1978	Barbara A. & Charles W. Switzer—Ch. Cede Higgins, Yorkshire Terrier
1979	Mrs. Anne E. Snelling—Ch. Oak Tree's Irishtocrat, Irish Water Spaniel
1980	Kathleen Kanzler—Ch. Innisfree's Sierra Cinnar, Siberian Husky
1981	Robert A. Hauslohner—Ch. Dhandys Favorite Woodchuck, Pug
1982	Mrs. Anne E. Snelling—Ch. St. Aubrey Dragonora of Elsdon, Pekingese
1983	Chris & Marguerite Terrell—Ch. Kabiks The Challenger, Afghan Hound
1984	Seaward Kennels, Reg.—Ch. Seaward's Blackbeard, Newfoundland
1985	Sonnie & Alan Novick—Ch. Braeburn's Close Encounter, Scottish Terrier
1986	Mrs. Alan R. Robson & Michael Zollo—Ch. Marjetta's National Acclaim, Pointer
1987	Shirlee Braunstein & Jane A. Firestone—Ch. Covy Tucker Hill's Manhattan, German Shepherd Dog
1988	Skip Piazza & Olga Baker—Ch. Great Elms Prince Charming, II, Pomeranian
1989	Richard & Carolyn Vida, Beth Wilhite & Arthur & Susan Korp—Ch. Royal Tudor's Wild As The Wind, Doberman Pinscher
1990	Edward B. Jenner—Ch. Wendessa Crown Prince, Pekingese
1991	Dr. & Mrs. Frederick Hartsock—Ch. Whisperwind On Carousel, Standard Poodle
1992	Marion W. & Samuel B. Lawrence—Ch. Registry's Lonesome Dove, Wire Fox Terrier
1993	Donna S. & Roger H. Herzig, MD, & Julia Gasow—Ch. Salilyn's Condor, English Springer Spaniel
1994	Ruth L. Cooper & Patricia P. Lussier-Forrest—Ch. Chidley Willum The Conqueror, Norwich Terrier
1995	Dr. Vandra L. Huber & Dr. Joe Kinnarny—Ch. Gaelforce Post Script, Scottish Terrier
1996	Richard & Judith Zaleski—Ch. Clussexx Country Sunrise, Clumber Spaniel
1997	Gabrio Del Torre and Rita Holloway—Ch. Parsifal Di Casa Netzer, Standard Schnauzer.

NATIONAL BREED CLUBS

For more information about a particular breed, please contact the following:

SPORTING GROUP

American Brittany Club, Inc. — Corres. Secretary, Joy Searcy, 800 Hillmont Ranch Road, Aldeo, TX 76008; Breeder Contact, Ms. Velma Tiedeman, 2036 N. 48th Ave., Omaha, NE 68104, (402) 553-5538.

American Pointer Club, Inc. — Secretary, Henri B. Tuthill, 20325 Magnolia Ave., Nuevo, CA 92567.

German Shorthaired Pointer Club of America — Secretary, Mary Beth Kirkland, 9702 Gayton Rd. #309, Richmond, VA 23233-4907; Breeder Contact, Ann King, 11946 NYS Rt. #34N, Cato, NY 13033, (315) 626-2990.

German Wirehaired Pointer Club of America, Inc. — Corres. Secretary, Karen Nelsen, 25821 Lucille Ave., Lomita, CA 90717; Breeder Contact, Mrs. Nancy Mason, 826 Cinebar Rd., Cinebar, WA 98533, (360) 985-2776.

American Chesapeake Club, Inc. — Corres. Secretary, Nancy Boylan, 619 14th Place, Kenosha, WI 53140; Breeder Contact, American Chesapeake Club, P.O. Box 523, Florissant, MO 63032-0523, (314) 653-1718.

Curly-Coated Retriever Club of America — Corres. Secretary and Breeder Contact, Penny A.W. Sleeth, 16594 You Bet Road, Grass Valley, CA 95945-8662, (916) 272-4378.

Flat-Coated Retriever Society of America, Inc. — Recording Secretary, Kurt Anderson, 42 Drazen Drive, North Haven, CT 06473; Breeder Contact, Kathy Barton 5325 Ann Hackley Road, Fort Wayne, IN 46835-1413.

Golden Retriever Club of America — Secretary, Linda Willard, 10604 Spring Valley, Austin, TX 78736; Breeder Contact, Anne McGuire, (281) 861-0820.

Labrador Retriever Club, Inc. — Secretary, 12471 Pond Road, Burton, Ohio 44021.

English Setter Association of America, Inc. — Secretary and Breeder Contact, Mrs. Dawn S. Ronyak, 114 S. Burlington Oval Dr., Chardon, OH 44024, (216) 285-4531.

Gordon Setter Club of America, Inc. — Corres. Secretary, Nikki Maounis, P.O. Box 54, Washougal, WA 98671; Breeder Contact, Ms. Phyllis Tew, 9707 N. Kiowa Road, Parker, CO 80134, (303) 841-2015.

Irish Setter Club of America, Inc. — Corres. Secretary, Mrs. Marion Pahy, 16717 Ledge Falls, San Antonio, TX 78232-1808; Breeder Contact, Mrs. Marilee Larson, 27371 Whitmor, Pioneer, CA 95666, (209) 295-1666.

American Water Spaniel Club — Secretary, Patricia A St. Onge, 4835 S. Mill Loop Rd., Maple, WI 54854-9011; Breeder Contact, Madie Kolk, 16542 James St., Holland, MI 49424, (800) 555-2972.

Clumber Spaniel Club of America, Inc. — Secretary, Ms. Barbara Stebbins, 2271 SW Almansa Ave, Port St. Lucie, FL 34953; Breeder Contact, Edythe Donovan, 241 Monterey Ave., Pelham, NY 10803, (914) 738-3976.

American Spaniel Club, Inc. — Corres. Secretary, Margaret M. Ciezkowski, 846 Old Stevens Creek Rd., Martinez, GA 30907-9227; Breeder Contact, Dorothy Mustard, 30 Cardinal Loop, Crossville, TN 38555, (615) 484-5434.

English Cocker Spaniel Club of America, Inc. — Secretary and Breeder Contact, Kate D. Romanksi, P.O. Box 252, Hales Corners, WI 53130, (414) 529-9714.

English Springer Spaniel Field Trial Association, Inc. — Corres. Secretary and Breeder Contact, Ms. Karen Koopman, 347 5th Ave., #1406, New York, NY 10016, (212) 481-7792.

Field Spaniel Society of America — Corres. Secretary, Becki Jo Wolkenheim, P.O. Box 187, Wales, WI 53183; Breeder Contact, Sharon Douthit, 1905 Ave. J. , Sterling, IL 61081, (815) 625-0467.

Irish Water Spaniel Club of America — Secretary and Breeder Contact, Renae Peterson, 24712 SE 380th St., Enumclaw, WA 98022-8833, (360) 825-6128.

Sussex Spaniel Club of America — Corres. Secretary, Sue Caniff, 2435 E. Aldine, Phoenix, AX 85032; Breeder Contact, Ms. Kathy Miller, 422 Ward Ave., Girard, OH 44420 (330) 545-6996.

Welsh Springer Spaniel Club of America, Inc. — Corres. Secretary, Karen Lyle, 4425 N. 147th St. Brookfield, WI 53005-1608; Breeder Contact, Pat Pencak, 135 Old Forrestburg Rd., Sparrow Bush, NY 12780, (914) 856-4533.

Vizsla Club of America, Inc. — Corres. Secretary and Breeder Contact, Mrs. Florence Duggan, 451 Longfellow Ave., Westfield, NJ 07090, (908) 789-9774.

Weimaraner Club of America — Corres. Secretary, Marge Davis, 13188 Flamingo Terr., Lake Park, FL 33410; Breeder Contact, Ms. Rebecca Weimer, 324 Sundew Dr., Belleville, IL 62221, (618) 236-1466.

American Wirehaired Pointing Griffon Association — Corres. Secretary, Barbara Ettrich, 8 Nelson Ave., Latham, NY 12110; Breeder Contact, Suzzette Wood, 3056 Partin Settlement Rd., Kissimee, FL 34744, (407) 846-0484.

HOUND GROUP

Afghan Hound Club of America — Corres. Secretary and Breeder Contact, Norma Cozzoni, 43 W. 612 Tall Oaks Trl. Elburn, IL 60119, (708) 365-3647.

Basenji Club of America — Secretary, Anne L. Graves, 5102 Darnell, Houston, TX 77096-1404; Breeder Contact, Melody Russell, 2714 NE 110th St., Seattle, WA 98125, (206) 362-4202.

Basset Hound Club of America, Inc. — Secretary and Breeder Contact, Melody Fair, P.O. Box 339, Noti, OR 97461, (541) 935-1672, fax: (541) 484-5881.

National Beagle Club — Secretary, Susan Mills Stone, 2555 Pennsylvania NW, Washington, DC 20037; Breeder Contact, Patricia Staub, 3 Rosehaven St., Stafford, VA 22554, (540) 752-0507.

American Black and Tan Coonhound Club — Secretary, Stan Bielowicz, 7222 Pate Rogers Rd., Fleming, GA 31309; Breeder Contact, Cheryl Speed, 3508 Berger Rd., Lutz, FL 33549, (813) 963-2033.

American Bloodhound Club — Secretary and Breeder Contact, Ed Kilby, 1914 Berry Ln., Daytona Beach, FL 32124, (904) 756-0373.

Borzoi Club of America, Inc. — Corres. Secretary and Breeder Contact, Karen Mays, 29 Crown Dr., Warren, NJ 07059-5111, (908) 647-3027.

Dachshund Club of America, Inc. — Secretary, Mr. Walter M. Jones, 390 Eminence Pike, Shelbyville, KY 40065; Breeder Contact, Mrs. Dorothy Hutchinson, East Woods Rd., Pound Ridge, NY 10576, (914) 764-5226.

Greyhound Club of America — Corres. Secretary and Breeder Contact, Margaret Bryson,15079 Meeting House Ln , Montpelier, VA 23192, (804) 883-7800.

Harrier Club of America — Secretary and Breeder Contact, Kimberly Mitchell, 301 Jefferson Lane, Ukiah, CA 95482, (707) 463-0501.

Ibizan Hound Club of the United States — Secretary, Jeffrey Macek, 2536 E. Whitton Ave., Phoenix, AZ 85016-7422; Breeder Contact, Lisa Puskas, 4312 E. Nisbet Rd., Phoenix, AZ 85032, (602) 493-7080.

Irish Wolfhound Club of America — Secretary and Breeder Contact, Mrs. William S. Pfarrer, 8855 U.S. Route 40, New Carlisle, OH 45344, (937) 845-9135.

Norwegian Elkhound Association of America, Inc. — Corres. Secretary and Breeder Contact, Debra Walker, 3650 Bay Creek Rd., Loganville, GA 30249, (770) 466-9967.

Otterhound Club of America — Corres. Secretary and Breeder Contact, Dian Quist-Sulek, Rt.#1, Box 247, Palmyra, NE 68418, (412) 799-3535.

Petit Basset Griffon Vendeen Club of America — Secretary and Breeder Contact, Ms. Shirley Knipe, 426 Laguna Way, Simi Valley, CA 93065, (805) 527-6327.

Pharaoh Hound Club of America — Corres. Secretary and Breeder Contact, Rita L. Sacks. P.O. Box 895454, Leesburg, FL 34789-5454, (352) 357-8723.

Rhodesian Ridgeback Club of the United States, Inc. — Corres. Secretary, Betty J. Epperson, P.O. Box 121817, Ft. Worth, TX 76121-1817; Breeder Contact, Jacque Rex, 25198 E. 19th St., San Bernardino, CA 92404, (909) 381-3064.

Saluki Club of America — Secretary, Donna J. Kappmeier, 12192 Gilbert St., Garden Grove, CA 92641; Breeder Contact, Ms. Cloris Costigan, 7 Huntington Rd., East Brunswick, NJ 08816, (908) 257-9134.

Scottish Deerhound Club of America, Inc. — Secretary, Mrs. Joan Shagan, 545 Cummings Ln., Cottontown, TN 37048; Breeder Contact, Ms. Bette Stencil, 1328 S. Riverside Ave., St. Claire, MI 48079-5133, (810) 329-3841.

American Whippet Club, Inc. — Secretary and Breeder Contact, Mrs. Harriet Nash Lee, 14 Oak Cir., Charlottesville, VA 22901, (804) 295-4525.

WORKING GROUP

Akita Club of America — Secretary, Anne Marie Taylor, 8083 Turner Rd., Fenton, MI 48430; Breeder Contact, Mrs. Debbie Stewart, 17945 Jo Ann Way, Perris, CA 92570-8961, (909) 943-1811.

Alaskan Malamute Club of America, Inc. — Corres. Secretary, Stephen Piper, 3528 Pin Hook Road, Antioch, TN 37013-1510; Breeder Contact, Cap Schneider, 21 Unneberg Ave., Succasunna, NJ 07876, (201) 584-7125.

Bernese Mountain Dog Club of America, Inc. — Secretary, Ms. Roxanne Bortnick, P.O. Box 270692, Fort Collins, CO 80527; Breeder Contact, Ms. Ruth Reynold, 5265 E. Fort Rd., Greenwood, FL 32443, (904) 594-4636.

American Boxer Club, Inc. — Corres. Secretary, Mrs. Barbara E. Wagner, 6310 Edward Dr., Clinton, MD 20735-4135; Breeder Contact, Mrs. Lucille Jackson, 11300 Oakton Rd., Oakton, VA 22124, (703) 385-9385.

American Bullmastiff Association, Inc. — Secretary, Linda Silva, 15 Woodland Lane, Smithtown, NY 11787; Breeder Contact, Ms. Barbara Brooks-Worrell, BR 16045 SE 296th, Kent, WA 98042.

Doberman Pinscher Club of America — Corres. Secretary, Nancy Jewell, 13451 N. Winchester Way., Parker, CO 80134; Breeder Contact, Mrs. Tommie F. Jones, 4840 Thomasville Rd., Tallahassee, FL 32308, (904) 668-1735.

Giant Schnauzer Club of America, Inc. — Secretary and Breeder Contact, Robin Greenslade, 12 Walnut Ter., Salem, NH 03079, (603) 894-4938.

Great Dane Club of America, Inc. — Corres. Secretary, Kathy Jurin, 1825 Oaklyn Dr. Green Lane, PA 18054; Breeder Contact, "Pookie" Kostuk, P.O. Box 2015, Cheshire, CT 06410, (203) 272-8292.

Great Pyrenees Club of America, Inc. — Corres. Secretary, Maureen Maxwell-Simon, 7430 Jonestown, Harrisburg, PA 17112; Breeder Contact, Janet Ingram, 204 Wild Partridge Ln., Radford, VA 24141, (540) 731-0299.

Komondor Club of America, Inc. — Corres. Secretary and Breeder Contact, Linda Patrick, 44601 Robson Belleville, MI 48111, (313) 699-8440.

Greater Swiss Mountain Dog Club of America, Inc. — Corres. Secretary, DeAnne Gerner, 91 Schoffers Rd., Reading, PA 19606.

Kuvasz Club of America — Corres. Secretary, Susan Gilmore, P.O. Box 90, Braceville, IL 60407; Breeder Contact, Pat Zupan, 2706 Garfield St., Wall Township, NJ 07719, (908) 681-3096.

Mastiff Club of America, Inc. — Corres. Secretary, Karen McBee, Rt.#7, Box 520, Fairmont, WV 26554; Breeder Contact, Ms. Carla Sanchez, 45935 Via Esperanza, Temecula, CA 92590, (203) 966-4253.

Newfoundland Club of America, Inc. — Corres. Secretary, Sandee Lovett 5870 5 Mile Rd. NE, Ada, MI 49301 Breeder Contact, Rebecca Cieniewicz, 341 Carter's Gin Rd., Toney, AL 35773 (205) 852-7015

Portuguese Water Dog Club of America, Inc. — Corres. Secretary, Cheryl G. Smith, 116 Teresita Way, Los Gatos, CA 95032; Breeder Contact, Arlene Gordon, 5051 E. Orchid Lane, Paradise Valley, AZ 85253, (602) 948-0118, fax (602)991-9338.

American Rottweiler Club — Corres. Secretary, Doreen LePage, 960 S. Main St., Pascoag, RI 02859; Breeder Contact, Lauri Ladwig, 1184 E. Fleetwood Ct., Boise, ID 83706, (208) 384-9881.

St. Bernard Club of America, Inc. — Corres. Secretary, Cheryl Zappala, 1043 S. 140th, Seattle, WA 98168, (206) 242-7480.

Samoyed Club of America, Inc. — Corres. Secretary and Breeder Contact, Lori Elvera, 3711 Brices Ford Ct., Fairfax, VA 22033, (703) 476-0735.

Siberian Husky Club of America, Inc. — Corres. Secretary, Mrs. Fain B. Zimmerman, 210 Madera Dr., Victoria, TX 77905-0611; Breeder Contact, Ms. Sandra Jessop, 152 Hemstead Ave., Malverne, NY 11565, (516) 887-7189.

Standard Schnauzer Club of America — Secretary, Liz Hansen, P.O. Box 153, Kampsville, IL 62053; Breeder Contact, Darlene Cornell, P.O. Box 87, Wappinger Falls, NY 12590, (914) 838-9207.

TERRIER GROUP

Airedale Terrier Club of America — Corres. Secretary, Dr. Suzanne Hampton, 47 Tulip Ave., Ringwood, NJ 07456; Breeder Contact, Corally Burmaster, 20146 Gleedsville Rd, Leesburg, VA 20175, (703) 779-8030.

Staffordshire Terrier Club of America — Secretary, Mr. H. Richard Pascoe, 785 Valley View Rd., Forney, TX 75126.

Australian Terrier Club of America, Inc. — Corres. Secretary, Ms. Marilyn Harban, 1515 Davon Ln., Nassau Bay, TX 77058; Breeder Contact, Mrs. Barbara Deer, 1868 Hovsons Blvd., Toms

River, NJ 08753, (908) 255-7594.
Bedlington Terrer Club of America — Corres. Secretary, Mr. Robert Bull, P.O. Box 11, Morrison, IL 61270-7419; Breeder Contact, Mr. Robert Bull, P.O. Box 11, Morrison, IL 61270-7419, (815) 772-4832.
Border Terrier Club of America, Inc. — Secretary, Pattie Pfeffer, 801 Los Luceros Dr. Eagle, ID 83616; Breeder Contact, Judy Donaldson, 135 Westledge Rd., W. Simsbury, CT 06092, (203) 651-0140.
Bull Terrier Club of America — Corres. Secretary and Breeder Contact, Mrs. Becky Poole, 2630 Gold Point Cir., Hixson, TN 37343, (423) 842-2611.
Cairn Terrier Club of America — Corres. Secretary and Breeder Contact, Christine M. Bowlus, 8096 Chilson Rd., Pinckney, MI 48169, (810) 231-4147.
Dandie Dinmont Terrier Club of America, Inc. — Secretary, Mrs. Gail Isner, 151 Junaluska Dr., Woodstock, GA 30188; Breeder Contact, Mrs. Lloyd Brewer, 1016 Mars Dr., Colorado Springs, 80906, (719) 473-9560.
American Fox Terrier Club — Secretary and Breeder Contact, Mr. Martin Goldstein, P.O. Box 604, South Plainfield, NJ 07080-0604, (908) 668-0715
Irish Terrier Club of America — Corres. Secretary, Cory Rivera, 22720 Perry St., Perris, CA 92570; Breeder Contact, Jeanne Burrage, 103 N. Frazier Ave., Florence, CO 81226, (719) 784-0931.
United States Kerry Blue Terrier Club, Inc. — Corres. Secretary, Mrs. Walter Fleisher, 443 Buena Vista Rd., New City, NY 10956; Breeder Contact, Lisa Frankland, 690 Korina St.,Vandenberg AFB, CA 93437, (805) 734-1280.
United States Lakeland Terrier Club — Secretary and Breeder Contact, Mrs. Edna Lawicki, 8207 E. Cholla St., Scottsdale, AZ 85260, (602) 998-8409.
American Manchester Terrier Club — Secretary, Ms. Sandra Kipp, Box 231,Gilbertville, IA 50634; Breeder Contact, Ms. Diana Haywood, 52 Hampton Rd., Pittstown, NJ 08867, (908) 996-7309.
Miniature Bull Terrier Club of America — Corres. Secretary, Kathy Brosnan, P.O. Box 634, Kingston, NH 03848; Breeder Contact, Susan Hall, 5641 Mount Gilead Rd., Centreville, VA 22020, (703) 631-3565.
American Miniature Schnauzer Club, Inc. — Secretary, Wyoma Clouss, 1932 Sunrise Rim Road, Boise, ID 83705; Breeder Contact, Amy Gordon, 3749 Victoria Dr., W. Palm Beach, FL 33406, (407) 964-4497.
Norwich and Norfolk Terrier Club — Corres. Secretary, Heidi H. Evans, 158 Delaware Ave., Laurel, DE 19956; Breeder Contact, Mrs. Susan Ely, 85 Mountain Top Rd., Bernardsville, NJ 07924, (908) 766-3468.
Scottish Terrier Club of America — Corres. Secretary and Breeder Contact, Evelyn D. Kirk, 2603 Derwent Dr. SW, Roanoke, VA 24015, (703) 345-2998.
American Sealyham Terrier Club — Secretary, Judy E. Thill, 13948 N. Cascade Rd., Dubuque, IA 52003; Breeder Contact, Mrs. Patsy Underwood, 3206 W Cortez Ct, Irving, TX 75062, (214) 255-3581.
Skye Terrier Club of America — Secretary, Ms. Maida Connor, 7 Fox Hill Avenue, Bristol, RI 02809; Breeder Contact, Donna C. Dale, 180 Marsh Creek Road, Gettysburg, PA 17325, (717) 334-0303, fax (717) 334-0710.
Soft Coated Wheaten Terrier Club of America — Corres. Secretary, John Giles, 15805 Honolulu, Houston, TX 77040; Breeder Contact, Mrs. Elaine Nerrie, 1945 Edgewood Rd., Redwood City, CA 94062, (415) 299-8778.
Staffordshire Bull Terrier Club, Inc. — Corres. Secretary, Catherine Swain, P.O. Box 5382, Montecito, CA 93150; Breeder Contact, Marilyn Atwood, 24451 Dartmouth, Dearborn Heights., MI 48125, (313) 277-3716.
Welsh Terrier Club of America, Inc. — Corres. Secretary and Breeder Contact, Derry Coe, 9967 E. Ida Ave., Greenwood Village, CO 80111, (303) 721-3334.
West Highland White Terrier Club of America — Corres. Secretary, Judith White, 8124 Apple Church Road, Thurmont, MD 21788, (301) 271-3380; Breeder Contact, Gale McDonald 3502 NW Half Mile Rd., Silverdale, WA 98383, 0-700-4WESTIE (AT&T access).

TOY GROUP

Affenpinscher Club of America — Secretary, Sharon I. Strempski, 2 Tucktaway Ln., Danbury, CT 06810; Breeder Contact, Ronald Carlson, 6114 Oliver Ave. S, Minneapolis, MN 55416, (612) 866-9606.
American Brussels Griffon Association — Secretary and Breeder Contact, Terry J. Smith, P.O. Box 56, Grand Ledge, MI 48837, (517) 627-5916.
American Cavalier King Charles Spaniel Club — Secretary, Martha Guimond, 1905 Upper Ridge Rd., Green Lane, PA 18054; Breeder Contact, Yarrow Morgan, 5506 Trading Post Trail South, Afton, MN 55001, (612) 436-8326.
Chihuahua Club of America, Inc. — Corres. Secretary, Lynnie Bunten, 5019 Village Trl., San Antonio, TX 78218; Breeder Contact, Josephine DeMenna, 2 Maple St., Wilton, CT 06897, (203) 762-2314.
American Chinese Crested Club, Inc. — Corres. Secretary and Breeder Contact, Kathleen Forth, Rt. 3 Box 157, Decatur, TX 76234, (817) 627-6772.
English Toy Spaniel Club of America — Corres. Secretary, Ms. Susan Jackson, 18451 Sheffield Ln., Bristol, IN 46507-9455; Breeder Contact, Ms. Christine Thaxton, 801 Greenwood Ave., Waukegan, IL 60087, (708) 662-1000.
Italian Greyhound Club of America, Inc. — Corres. Secretary and Breeder Contact, Lilian Barber, 35648 Menifee Rd., Murrieta, CA 92563, (909) 679-5084.
Japanese Chin Club of America — Secretary, Barbara Vallance, 1047 N. Stine Rd., Charlotte, MI 48813; Breeder Contact, Mrs. Charla Cross, 3321 Huntleigh Dr., Raleigh, NC 27604, (919) 876-9336.
American Maltese Association, Inc. — Corres. Secretary and Breeder Contact, Pamela G. Rightmyer, 2211 S. Tioga Way, Las Vegas, NV 89117, (702) 256-0420.
American Manchester Terrier Club — Secretary, Sandra Kipp, 5244 Rottinghaus Rd. Rt. 7, Waterloo, IA 50701; Breeder Contact, Ms. Diana Haywood, 52 Hampton Rd., Pittstown, NJ 08867, (908) 996-7309.
Miniature Pinscher Club of America, Inc. — Secretary, Vivian A. Hogan, 26915 Clarksburg Rd., Damascus, MD 20872; Breeder Contact, Glory Ann Pigarut, 9600 Massie Dr., Clinton, MD 20735, (301) 868-2997.
Papillon Club of America, Inc. — Corres. Secretary and Breeder Contact, Mrs. Janice Dougherty, 551 Birch Hill Rd., Shoemakersville, PA 19555, (610) 926-5581.
Pekingese Club of America, Inc. — Secretary, Mrs. Leonie Marie Schultz, Rt. #1, Box 321, Bergton, VA 22811; Breeder Contact, Mrs. Judith Pomato, 535 Devils Ln., Ballston Spa, NY 12020, (518) 885-6864.
American Pomeranian Club, Inc. — Corres. Secretary, Brenda Turner, 3910 Concord Place, Texarkana, TX 75501-2212; Breeder Contact, Jane Lehtinen, 1325 9th St. S, Virginia, MN 55792, (218) 741-2117.
Poodle Club of America, Inc. — Corres. Secretary and Breeder Contact, Mr. Charles Thomasson, 503 Martineau Dr., Chester, VA 23831-5753, (804) 530-1605.
Pug Dog Club of America, Inc. — Secretary, Mr. James P. Cavallaro, 1820 Shadowlawn St., Jacksonville, FL 32205; Breeder Contact, Mary Ann Hall, 15988 Kettington Road., Chesterfield, MO 63017-7350, (314) 207-1508.
American Shih Tzu Club, Inc. — Corres. Secretary, Bonnie Prato, 5252 Shafter Ave., Oakland, CA 94618; Breeder Contact, Andy Warner, 2 Big Oak Rd., Dillsburg, PA 17019, (717) 432-4351.
Silky Terrier Club of America, Inc. — Secretary and Breeder Contact, Ms. Louise Rosewell, 2783 S. Saulsbury St., Denver, CO 80227, (303) 988-4361.
Yorkshire Terrier Club of America, Inc. — Secretary and Breeder Contact, Mrs. Shirley A. Patterson, 2 Chestnut Ct., Star Rt. Pottstown, PA 19464, (610) 469-6781.

NON-SPORTING GROUP

American Eskimo Dog Club of America — Corres. Secretary, Barbara Beynon, 473 University Dr., Corpus Christi, TX 78414; Breeder Contact, Carolyn Jester, Rt #3 Box 211B, Stroud, OK 74079, (918) 968-3358.
Bichon Frise Club of America, Inc. — Corres. Secretary, Mrs. Bernice D. Richardson, 186 Ash Street, N. Twin Falls, ID 83301; Breeder Contact, Jane Lagemann, Hounds Ridge Rd., Lewisville, NC 27023, (910) 945-9788.
Boston Terrier Club of America — Corres. Secretary, Marian Sheehan, 8537 E. San Burno Drive, Scottsdale, AZ 85258; Breeder Contact, Patricia Stone, 14792 Ronda Dr., San Jose, CA 95124, (408) 371-7452.
Bulldog Club of America — Secretary, Toni Stevens, P.O. Box 248, Nobleton, FL 34661; Breeder Contact, Susan Rodenski, 480 Bully Hill Dr., King George, VA 22485, (703) 775-3015.
Chinese Shar-Pei Club of America, Inc. — Secretary, Judy Dorough, 9806 Mission Blvd., Riverside, CA 92509; Breeder Contact, Jocelyn Barker, P.O. Box 113809, Anchorage, AK 99511, (907) 345-6504.
Chow Chow Club, Inc. — Corres. Secretary, Irene Cartabio, 3580 Plover Pl., Seaford, NY 11783; Breeder Contact, David Neilsen, Rt #5 Box 563, Winnsboro, SC 29180, (803) 635-7047.
Dalmatian Club of America, Inc. — Corres. Secretary, Mrs. Sharon Boyd, 1303 James St., Rosenberg, TX 77471; Breeder Contact, Mrs. Gerri Lightholder, 6109 W. 147th St., Oak Forest, IL 60452, (708) 687-5447.
Finnish Spitz Club of America — Secretary, Bill Storz, 34 Sunrise Drive., Baltic, CT 06330; Breeder Contact, Sheila Goodwin, 57 Whitney Drive, South Fork Road, Cody, WY 82414, (307) 527-4835.
French Bulldog Club of America — Corres. Secretary, Diana H. Young, 5451 Vance Jackson Rd., San Antonio, TX 78230; Breeder Contact, Mr. Harry Dunn, Jr., 3638 Mayfair Dr., Tuscaloosa, AL 35404-5408, (205) 553-3817.
Keeshond Club of America, Inc. — Corres. Secretary, Tawn Sinclair, 11782 Pacific Coast Hwy. Malibu, CA 90265; Breeder Contact, Pat Yagecic, 4726 B Grant Ave., Philadelphia, PA 19114, (215) 637-7731.
American Lhasa Apso Club, Inc. — Secretary, Amy Andrews, 18105 Kirkshire, Beverly Hills, MI 48025.
Poodle Club of America, Inc. — Corres. Secretary, Mr. Charles Thomasson, 503 Martineau Dr., Chester, VA 23831-5753.
Schipperke Club of America, Inc. — Corres. Secretary, Dawn Hribar, 70480 Morency, Romeo, MI 48065; Breeder Contact, Margi Brinkley, 3245 8th St. S, Lebanon, OR 97355, (541) 259-3826.
National Shiba Club of America — Corres. Secretary, Kim Carlson, 526 Orchid Ct., Benicia, CA 94510; Breeder Contact, Jacey Holden, 3991 W. Peltier Rd., Lodi, CA 95242, (209) 369-3473.
Tibetan Spaniel Club of America — Corres. Secretary and Breeder Contact, Valerie Robinson, 103 Old Colony Dr., Mashpee, MA 02649, (508) 477-9637.
Tibetan Terrier Club of America — Secretary, Sharon Harrison, P.O. Box 528, Pleasanton, TX 78064; Breeder Contact, Mrs. Trudy Erceg, 356 Laurel Park Pl., Hendersonville, NC 28791, (704) 692-5007.

HERDING GROUP

Australian Cattle Dog Club of America — Secretary and Breeder Contact, Katherine Buetow, 2003B Melrose Drive, Champaign, IL 61820, (217) 359-0284.
United States Australian Shepherd Association — Secretary, Andrea Blizard, 34 Deckertown Tpke., Sussex, NJ 07461.
Bearded Collie Club of America, Inc. — Corres. Secretary and Breeder Contact, Kathy Finley, 3232 E. Helena Dr., Phoenix, AZ 85032, (602) 992-1899.
American Belgian Malinois Club — Corres. Secretary, Susan Morse, 7 Sunset West Circle, Ithaca, NY 14850; Breeder Contact, Sharon Burke, 11605 Highview Ave., Wheaton, MD 20902, (301) 946-0195.
Belgian Sheepdog Club of America, Inc. — Corres. Secretary and Breeder Contact, Marilyn Russell, RFD 2, Box 2480, Bangor, ME 04401, (207) 848-5613.
American Belgian Tervuren Club, Inc. — Corres. Secretary and Breeder Contact, Karen Johnson, P.O. Box 174, Walled Lake, MI 48390, (810) 685-3648.
Border Collie Society of America — Corres. Secretary, Richard Whorton, 815 Royal Oaks, Durham, NC 27712.
American Bouvier des Flandres Club, Inc. — Corres. Secretary and Breeder Contact, Dorothy Kent, 10520 West 102nd Place, Westminster, CO 80021, (303) 466-1242.
Briard Club of America, Inc. — Secretary, Sue Wahr, 1 Seneca Cir., Andover, MA 01810; Breeder Contact, Sharon Wise, 31 High St., Winthrop, ME 04364-1322, (207) 377-8689.
Collie Club of America, Inc. — Secretary and Breeder Contact, Carmen Leonard, 1119 South Fleming Rd, Woodstock, IL 60098, (815) 337-0323.
German Shepherd Dog Club of America, Inc. — Corres. Secretary and Breeder Contact, Blanche Beisswenger, 17 West Ivy Lane, Englewood, NJ 07631, (201) 568-5806.
Old English Sheepdog Club of America, Inc. — Corres. Secretary, Kathryn Bunnell, 14219 E. 79th St. S., Derby, KS 67037; Breeder Contact, Ms. Joan Long, 5704 Greenwood, Shawnee, KS 66216, (913) 631-5614.
Puli Club of America, Inc. — Secretary and Breeder Contact, Mrs. Patricia Giancaterino, 134 Mitchell Ave., Runnemede, NJ 08078, (609) 939-3096.
American Shetland Sheepdog Association — Corres. Secretary, Mr. George Page, 1100 Cataway Pl., Bryans Road, MD 20616; Breeder Contact, Mrs. Joyce Kern, 1879 Cole Rd., Aromas, CA 95004, (408) 726-1660.
Cardigan Welsh Corgi Club of America — Corres. Secretary, Ginny Conway, 14511 Trophey Club Dr., Houston, TX 77095-3420; Breeder Contact, Tricia Olson, 5512 La Plata Cir., Boulder, CO 80301, (303) 530-7107.
Pembroke Welsh Corgi Club of America, Inc. — Corres. Secretary and Breeder Contact, Joan Gibson Reid, 9589 Sheldon Rd., Elk Grove, CA 95624, (916) 689-1661.

INDEX